# RHINELANDERS ON THE YADKIN

The Story of the Pennsylvania Germans
in Rowan and Cabarrus

By

CARL HAMMER, JR., M.A., Ph.D.

Member of the Department of German
Vanderbilt University

*"And the rain descended, and the
floods came, and the winds blew, and
beat upon that house: and it fell not,
for it was founded upon a rock."*—
MATTH. 7:25

Southern Historical Press, Inc.
Greenville, South Carolina

*To my parents, always my companions in the study of local history.*

This volume was reproduced from
an 1943 edition located in the
Publisher's private Library

**Please Direct All Correspondence and Book Orders to:**

**Southern Historical Press, Inc.**
**1071 Park West Blvd.**
**Greenville, SC    29611**

Originally printed: Salisbury, NC  1943
ISBN #978-1-63914-250-7
*Printed in the United States of America*

# FOREWORD

The inspiration for this book dates from 1931, when the author's father encountered a speaker of the old German dialect, even then nearly extinct about here. From that first informant the writer learned of others who still remembered some of the almost-forgotten language; thereupon he resolved to save the last remnants of it from oblivion.

A paper read before a linguistic society in 1935 met with such a favorable response that the author felt encouraged to widen the scope of his research to include the historical background of the local Pennsylvania German element. The years since have brought a vast accumulation of data, which has been thoroughly sifted in an effort to produce a concise, yet definitive history of the Rhenish settlements in Rowan and Cabarrus Counties.

Footnotes acknowledge specific indebtedness to books or pamphlets; general mention is here made of articles in the *Salisbury Post* by Edith Clark, C. A. Daniel, and John Harden; in the *Carolina Watchman* by G. H. Cox, D.D., and Z. A. Kluttz; in the *Charlotte Observer* by W. M. Sherrill and Marion Wright; in the *New Yorker Staats-Zeitung und Herold* by H. M. Hoffmann and A. Rupp. Thanks are due to the following people for help in collecting material: Miss Agnes Walton, Messrs. J. L. Fisher, M. L. Stirewalt, D. D., John Harden, S. Holmes Plexico, Hoyle Bostian, and Marvin Webb. The unfailing assistance and encouragement of Professor John G. Frank, of Vanderbilt University, claim especially grateful recognition.

The transcription of the dialect is original, and all translations accompanying records or inscriptions are the work of the writer. He hopes that the following pages reflect in some degree his life-long acquaintance with the scenes described therein.

# CONTENTS

# ILLUSTRATIONS

# CHAPTER I

## THE EXODUS FROM THE HOMELAND

There is an inescapable charm about the gently rolling landscape of southeastern Rowan and the neighboring part of Cabarrus. Standing upon almost any rise, one looks out over well-kept farms and pasturelands, amid a setting of wooded hills and peacefully flowing streams. Now gazing eastward, far across the broad valley of the Yadkin, the eye is enraptured by the blue Uwharries.

An atmosphere of quiet beauty and repose abides there, as if offering a refuge to all who are weary of the tumultuous world outside. So it must likewise have seemed to those men and women who, about the middle of the eighteenth century, chose this region as a home for themselves and their children's children. Not only was their new country surpassingly fair, but it also afforded many a vista reminiscent of the distant homeland. It was a long, toilsome way from the Rhine provinces to piedmont Carolina, and the story of that migration has its beginnings— at an earlier period—in some of the most tragic events of European history.

The Thirty Years' War in Germany brought such desolation that some sections hardly recovered before the lapse of two centuries.[1] It was a long series of bloody conflicts and endless depredations that brought inconceivable ruin and abject human misery in their train. Only scant alleviation came through the Peace of Westphalia: marauding bands still roamed the countryside, robbing and murdering a large percentage of whatever peasants had somehow managed to survive the scourge of the Imperial troops on the one hand, and of the Swedes on the other. Certain areas lost no less than three-fourths of their population during the war and its aftermath.

Hardly any part of Germany had suffered worse from the repeated devastations than that beautiful province on the left bank of the Rhine known as the Palatinate. There and in the adjoining Rhenish territories the luckless inhabitants endured untold horrors of starvation, disease, and torture. The lovely old university town of Heidelberg fell a victim to the Catholic armies of Count Tilly (chiefly infamous for his butchery at Magdeburg), who plundered the priceless library and presented his loot to the Pope.

No section, however, was quicker to recover in some measure than the fertile, sunny Rhineland, with its industrious farmers and artisans. Even the sorely-tried Palatinate took new hope when the Elector Karl Ludwig, son of the unfortunate "Winter King," as-

1. Cf. Freytag: *Bilder aus der deutschen Vergangenheit*, III, 234 ff.

cended the throne. This wise and benevolent ruler accomplished much for the social and material betterment of his land, but the disaster was too great to be repaired in a short while. Another chain of misfortunes was already taking shape—a succession of terrors which were to surpass even those of the religious wars.

King Louis XIV, of France, "le Grand Monarque," seeing that Germany was prostrate, disunited, and threatened by the Turks in Hungary, thought the moment opportune for ravaging and burning extensive districts along the Rhine.[2] The pillaging of some sections was repeated so often that the inhabitants did not dare cultivate their fields for three years. Unable to defend his realm, the hapless Elector was forced to pay tribute to the "most Christian King" of the French. Karl Ludwig died in 1680, the very year in which another incursion took place. Under his unworthy successors, the people were entirely at the mercy of Louis. The brutal attacks of 1674 and 1680 formed a mere prelude to the cruelest invasion of all, which Louis began in 1688, again with no declaration of war. This time he based his action on a preposterous claim to the Palatinate through "inheritance," because the late elector's daughter, Elisabeth Charlotte ("Liselotte"), had married the Duke

2. Cf. Einhart: *Deutsche Geschichte* (2nd Ed., Leipzig, 1910), 145 f.

of Orleans. The real purpose of the French king was to make the Rhine country a desert and keep it a barren waste, lest it serve as a granary and base of attack for his enemies, chiefly the Emperor Leopold and the Great Elector (of Brandenburg, which later became the Kingdom of Prussia). These two were joined by William III, of England, in a coalition which Louis hoped to nip in the bud.[3] In February, 1689, the Emperor declared war against France, thus officially aligning himself with a North German alliance of Brandenburg, Hanover, Saxony, and Hesse-Cassel. Early in that year the French, who had advanced far into German territory, were forced back to the Rhine; this retreat was the occasion for the very worst despoliation that the Rhenish provinces had to undergo.[4]

Central Europe experienced a bitterly cold winter in 1688-1689, and it was then that the city of Mannheim was burned and the splendid castle of Heidelberg was left partly in ruins. Not long afterward the same fate befell Worms and Speyer, once the scenes of imperial pomp and great prosperity.[5] The inhabitants of the smaller towns and countless villages fared even worse, as they fell more easily a prey to the greed and cruelty of the French troops. Nearly

---

3. Henderson: *A Short History of Germany,* II, 58f.
4. Heyck: *Deutsche Geschichte* (Leipzig, 1906), III, 191.
5. See K. Lamprecht: *Deutsche Geschichte* (3rd Ed., Berlin, 1911), VII, 500.

five hundred thousand Palatines were driven forth into the snow from their burning homes. Those who were not cut down by the enemy, or who escaped immediate death from the terrible cold, faced not only exile, but famine and pestilence.[6] Holland was the immediate refuge for whoever was able to flee the country. The seaports of the Netherlands and England formed the gateway to America. A German colony already established in Pennsylvania offered hope to the more venturesome souls among the survivors.

Finally, in 1707, came the War of the Spanish Succession, bringing destruction once more to the left bank of the Rhine. Again great numbers of the inhabitants were rendered homeless, and the impetus was given to a mass emigration involving thousands of Palatines. First among these were ten families, totaling sixty persons, under the leadership of the Lutheran pastor Josua von Kocherthal. They traveled by way of Holland to London, where Queen Anne received them with great kindness, appropriating a shilling a day for each one. On August 25, 1708, the refugees were naturalized as British subjects, prior to being sent as colonists to the Hudson Valley.[7] Still more of their countrymen joined them in time to set sail for New York, in company with Lord Lovelace,

6. Cf. A. B. Faust: *The German Element in the United States* (N. Y., 1927), I, 57 f.
7. Ibid., 74.

the new governor of the colony. Upon arriving, Lovelace assigned to the Germans a strip of land along Quassaic Creek, on the west bank of the Hudson, where they founded the town of Neuburg (Newburgh).

Both the queen and the governor remained constant in their friendship for these first Rhenish settlers in New York. The news of the royal magnanimity toward Kocherthal's party, along with glowing accounts of the Hudson region, soon reached the Rhineland and inspired thousands of oppressed people from the Palatinate and Swabia to migrate to the New World. Another contributing factor was the hard winter of 1708-1709, which killed crops, fruit trees, and grape vines, and even caused the newly-pressed wine to freeze in the casks. Konrad Weiser, then twelve years old, tells in his diary of the widespread dying of the animals and birds by reason of the fearful cold.[8]

Accordingly, in the spring of 1709, multitudes of Palatines journeyed down the Rhine on rafts and small boats to Rotterdam, where they took ship for London. By October about 14,000 of them had arrived in the English capital. Their large numbers caused some consternation: nevertheless, the Londoners at first showed themselves very charitable toward these homeless victims of war and religious

---

8.  Ibid., 76 f.

oppression. The newcomers were housed in vacant dwellings, warehouses, barns, even army tents, and an effort was made to provide them with food.[9] With the hardships of winter, death came to thousands; also, public interest inevitably began to wane. Hence the government felt obliged to take action. Several thousand immigrants, especially Catholics unwilling to turn Protestant, were shipped back to Holland and Germany, while 3800 were sent to work in the spinning mills of Ireland. A few hundred were quartered outside of London, under unsatisfactory conditions, and when they tried to escape by night, they were condemned to slavery in Jamaica.

Already in the autumn of 1709 a company of 600 Palatines and Swiss had left for Carolina, under the leadership of Christoph von Graffenried and Louis Michel, both natives of Switzerland. Accepting the liberal terms of the Lords Proprietors, the two bought 10,000 acres of land and arranged to have an additional 100,000 acres laid off and reserved for twelve years.[10] In 1710 the party arrived in two vessels at the confluence of the Neuse and Trent rivers and there founded Neu-Bern (New Bern). Sixty of the settlers perished the following year in the great massacre of the whites by the Tuscarora Indians. Furthermore, the Germans and Swiss fared ill at the hands of Graffenried, who withheld from them the

9. Ibid, 77 f.
10. Ibid., 212 f.

titles to their lands, which he and Michel sold to their own creditors; he then returned to Europe, deserting the victims of his speculation. The latter sent a petition to the Carolina Council in 1714, asking for a grant of 400 acres of land for each family and two years' time in which to pay for it. Their plea was granted, and the colony entered upon more prosperous days.[11]

In April, 1710, the great mass of Rhinelanders remaining in England—over 3,000 persons—sailed on ten ships to the New York colony. With them traveled the successor of the deceased Lord Lovelace, Colonel Hunter. Several hundred died in the course of a luckless voyage, and many more perished while being held in quarantine at Nutton (Governor's) Island. One vessel sank, and although the passengers were rescued, they lost all their belongings. Konrad Weiser relates that some Indian chiefs, on a visit in London, had been moved to pity by the plight of the exiled people and had promised them lands on the Schoharie River. But this prospect did not go beyond a commission sent by Governor Hunter to inspect the region in question. Meanwhile it had been decided in London that the Germans should be settled on the Hudson, where they were to produce naval supplies and serve as a check on the Indians and French.

11. Ibid., 214 f.

This venture proved unsuccessful and brought only added hardships to the disillusioned immigrants.[12]

The vicissitudes of the Palatines in New York are too many for a detailed treatment here. Unsympathetic governors and officials, animosity on the part of the long settled Dutch, the shameful greed and chicanery of the great landowners, particularly Robert Livingston, made their lot an almost unbearable one.[13] Part of them remained in the original settlement, or else went to the Mohawk Valley, while large companies (nearly two-thirds) moved southward to Pennsylvania at the invitation of Governor Keith. The first migration took place in the spring of 1723, under the leadership of Hartmann Windecker. A second large group, led by Konrad Weiser the Younger, followed in 1728. Thanks to their industry, the Germans were this time well equipped to begin life in a new territory.

Upon their arrival in Pennsylvania, the Rhinelanders found their compatriots already numerous. The first German (and Palatine) colony in America had been founded as early as 1683 by that versatile and picturesque character, Franz Daniel Pastorius, a young lawyer from Sommerhausen, with the aid and encouragement of William Penn. By means of translations of his pamphlets, the latter had appealed

12. Cf. Faust, 78.
13. Ibid., 84.

to the Pietists and Mennonites of Germany to take part in his experiment. While visiting Frankfurt-on-the-Main, Pastorius became intimate with Spener and other leaders of Pietism, who had just formed a land company and bought 15,000 acres for colonization in the Quaker Province.[14] Pastorius came as agent of the corporation and continued in that capacity until 1700, but throughout the rest of his life he remained the chief citizen of Germantown,[15] a settlement which he had established with singular success. There the first paper mill in America was built and the first Bible was printed by Christoph Sauer in 1743. Already in 1688 the people of Germantown made the earliest formal protest ever uttered in this country against Negro slavery.[16]

From 1683 till 1710, immigration proceeded slowly and in small numbers. After the latter date there was a substantial increase from year to year. Thus, when the Palatines came down from the Hudson Valley, large companies were arriving directly from the homeland. Comparatively few Germans landed in New York after the sad experience of the Rhenish colonists there; Baltimore and Charleston also received considerable numbers, but Philadelphia probably surpassed all the others combined, as a port of

14. Albert C. Myers: *Narratives of Early Pennsylvania* (N. Y., 1912), 355 ff.
15. Ibid.
16. Faust, 45 ff.

Courtesy of Mr. James L. Fisher.

TOWNHALL AND CHURCH AT FREINSHEIM IN THE PALATINATE

This quaint old town, near the ancient imperial city of Worms, was the home of the Fisher family before the migration to America.

entry for immigrants from the Fatherland before the Revolution.[17] By 1727 the influx became so great that the authorities began to keep records, giving the name of the person and usually the name of the country whence he came. It is estimated that 12,000 Germans reached Pennsylvania in the year 1749,[18] and that by 1775 there were 110,000 people of German birth or descent, or one-third of the total population of the province. Long before that date, however, they had settled, albeit in smaller numbers, in nearly every colony. Not all who came to Pennsylvania were natives of the Palatinate or even of neighboring provinces. Many were from more distant parts of Germany as well as from Switzerland. Nevertheless, the "Pfaelzer" were so numerous that the name was indiscriminately bestowed upon any German; thus we even read of a "Palatine from Holstein"![19] Likewise the word *Deutsch*, meaning "German," was mistaken for "Dutch"—an error perpetuated to this day.

And so began the mighty wave of German immigration, which was to reach its highest point during the nineteenth century. Conservative computations have shown that twenty-four to twenty-seven per

17. Ibid., 111.
18. A. D. Graeff: *The Relations Between the Pennsylvania Germans and the British Authorities* (1750-1776), (Norristown, 1939), 19.
19. Faust, 54.

cent of our white population is of German origin, as against thirty per cent of English extraction.[20] The exodus from the Palatinate was the most significant phase of the initial movement. Chief among the causes motivating this mass migration were: the destructive wars, religious persecutions, and oppression by tyrannical rulers at home; the extravagant accounts of a "promised land" which were circulated by the so-called "newlanders" (agents of ship companies and firms speculating in colonization schemes); finally, the hope of religious freedom that had been denied in Europe. These settlers in Pennsylvania and their descendants have been leaders in the important, but all-too little known role played by the German element in the development of our country.

The three principal religious denominations among the Pennsylvania Germans were: the Lutherans, with their great leader, Heinrich Melchior Muehlenberg; the German Reformed, whose chief organizer was Michael Schlatter; and the United Brethren, or Moravians, among whom the greatest name is that of Nicholas, Count Zinzendorf. Quite numerous were the adherents of such sects as the Mennonites, Dunkards, and Schwenkfelder. The Mennonites, so called after the founder of their faith, Menno Simons (1492-1559), of Friesland, bore many resemblances

20. V. H. Todd & Julius Goebel: *Christoph von Graffenried's Account of the Founding of Newbern* (N. C. Hist. Commission, 1920), 5.

to the Quakers in doctrine, as did also the Dunkards to some extent.[21]

In 1752 Schlatter estimated the number of his German Reformed followers at 30,000. At the same time, he conceded that they did not form over a third of the total German population of Pennsylvania. Muehlenberg placed the Lutheran membership at twice the figure for the Reformed Church, namely, at approximately 60,000 persons. If one assumes that the adherents of those two denominations numbered nearly 90,000, then, with the addition of some thousands of members of other sects, it becomes evident that the 100,000 mark had already been passed before that date.[22] At first glance this is surprising, in view of the fact that, as mentioned above, the Teutonic element in 1775 amounted to only about 110,000. The explanation is that a third or more of the Pennsylvania Germans and their natural increase left the colony, in the course of several decades, to settle in the alluring and spacious lands toward the South. Not only did long-established families, or their young people, strike out for new territory, but often recent arrivals from Germany made no more than a brief stop before journeying onward to other provinces. Thus Pennsylvania, aside from absorbing the greater part of the pre-revolutionary German immigration, also became the point of departure for less densely-populated regions of promise.

---

21. Faust, 112 ff.
22. Ibid., 129.

From the first settlements at Philadelphia and in the counties of Berks, Lancaster, and Montgomery, the Germans pushed northward and westward to Lehigh, Northampton, and Monroe, then to Lebanon and Dauphin. Crossing the Susquehanna, they settled also in the present counties of York, Cumberland, and Adams.[23] Southward from there, they could follow the mountain slopes through Maryland and into Virginia by way of the Shenandoah Valley, where many found permanent homes. Other large bodies continued their journey as far as central North Carolina, and to these we must now turn.

23. Ibid.

# CHAPTER II

## A LONG-SOUGHT HAVEN

It was more than a third of a century after the founding of Newbern that the second German migration to North Carolina began. The new movement brought largely Palatines also, but instead of coming directly from Europe, they trekked down from Pennsylvania, hauling their household and farm equipment in wagons and driving their livestock before them. Taking the Shenandoah route mentioned in the previous chapter, they followed the Staunton River through the Blue Ridge and then went southward across the Dan River to the Valley of the Yadkin.[1]

The principal cause of the removal to the South was the scarcity of land, which, even on the Pennsylvanian frontier, was available only in small amounts sold by the Indians. In the favored easterly sections the cost of farms was almost prohibitive.[2] Not until after the Revolution did the settlers venture across the Allegheny Mountains; their way led southward to the stretches of fertile soil in piedmont Carolina, where large tracts could be bought cheaply from the agents of the Earl of Granville.

---

1. *Colonial Records of North Carolina* (henceforth designated as C. R.), I, 22.
2. Faust, op. cit., 230.

Customarily and traditionally the year 1745 has been given as the date for the first appearance of the Germans in the interior of North Carolina. According to the scanty documentary evidence still extant, the Palatine colony in the present counties of Rowan and Cabarrus was founded somewhat later. Describing his visit to these parts in 1755, Governor Arthur Dobbs wrote (August 24th) : ". . . There are twenty-two families of Germans or Swiss, who are all an industrious people." Further on he refers to "their settlement seven or eight years ago."[3] Hence 1747 would seem to be more accurate than the earlier figure, as is also indicated by certain title-deeds, dated 1752, for lands already occupied about five years.

The inflow of Pennsylvania Germans came into full swing between 1750 and 1775; it continued, however, even after the Revolutionary War, covering therefore a period of about forty years. Moreover, these settlements embraced an extensive territory: namely, portions of Alamance, Orange, Guilford, Davidson, Rowan, Cabarrus, Stanly, Iredell, Wilkes, Catawba, Lincoln, and several other counties.

Another and entirely different group of Germans from Pennsylvania, the gentle and industrious Moravians, began to arrive in North Carolina in 1753. They settled in what is now Forsyth, on a large tract of land selected the preceding year by their beloved

3. C. R., V, 356.

and learned bishop, August Gottlieb Spangenberg. This settlement was called "Wachovia," in honor of Count Zinzendorf, lord of the Wachau Valley in Austria. The selection of the prospective colonists was made partly on the basis of their trades or professions.[4] Daily records, carefully kept by the Moravian Brethren, form an invaluable source of historical information, such as is unfortunately not to be found in the case of their near neighbors, the Palatines.

Simultaneously with the Germans, many Scotch-Irish came from Pennsylvania in search of new homes. The two peoples had lived on friendly terms in that province, and the harmonious relationship continued in North Carolina. Although they often settled side by side, a great number of the Scotch-Irish occupied vacant lands to the west or south of the Germans. Both took part, however, in the inevitable westward push, and eventually became about equally numerous in the valley of the Catawba River.[5]

Locally, we find the Germans thickest in southeastern Rowan, in the vicinity of Organ and Lowerstone churches, and in the adjoining section of Cabarrus, around "Old St. John's." To this day the descendants of the Rhinelanders predominate in that region, which also contains several noteworthy archi-

---

4.  Adelaide L. Fries: *Records of the Moravians in North Carolina* (Publ. N. C. Hist. Commission, 1922 ff.), 15.
5.  Cf. Faust, 228.

tectural monuments dating from the early decades of their settlement. There is no way of determining just how many of those people were born in Germany and how many were natives of Pennsylvania, even though in a few cases it is authentic that some of them actually came from "the Old Country." While probably not many survivors of the exodus of 1708 ever reached North Carolina, after a lapse of forty years, it must be remembered that thousands of Germans were landing yearly at Philadelphia during the period in question.

As a rule, the Germans left Pennsylvania in the fall as soon as their crops were gathered. Therefore they arrived in the South just before cold weather, well supplied with the means of passing through the winter without undue hardship.[6] By reason of their foresight, these colonists apparently experienced a minimum of frontier troubles. In a milder climate than they had ever known, it was relatively easy to build log houses that would afford them reasonable protection against the cold. At the coming of spring they were able to begin farming with favorable prospects for a good crop from the virgin soil. They had brought along enough livestock to assure them of an ample increase in their new environment.

"These German settlers," wrote Dr. Bernheim, "were all industrious, economical, and thrifty farm-

6. Ibid.

ers, not afraid nor ashamed of hard labor, and they were soon blessed with an abundance of everything which the fertile soil and temperate climate could furnish them. As they were . . . agriculturists, they generally avoided settling . . . in town."[7]

One must not suppose, however, that all the Germans held themselves entirely aloof from public life. Even in the earliest days a few began to assume their places as prominent and energetic citizens. Among these was John Lewis Beard. Evidently the tradition of his German birth is correct, for it is known that he was not naturalized until 1755, after coming (by way of Pennsylvania) to the newly-founded town of Salisbury. Having learned English quickly and well, he went into business and soon took an active part in the affairs of his adopted community, serving as town commissioner,[8] as a trustee of the "Salisbury Academy,"[9] and as a member of the Committee of Safety of 1775.[10]

Other well-known figures of German descent around Salisbury were Frederick Fischer (Fisher), also a business man, and Michael Braun (Brown).

---

7.  Gotthardt Dellmann Bernheim, D.D.: *History of the German Settlements and the Lutheran Church in North and South Carolina* (Philadelphia, 1872), 153.
8.  C. R., XXIII, 810.
9.  Ibid., XXIV, 690; Valentine Beard is also mentioned (loc. cit.) as a trustee.
10.  Ibid., X, 279 f. In 1790 Salisbury numbered fifty or sixty homes, of which ten were German, according to Velthusen (*Nordcarolinische Kirchennachrichten*, 16).

The latter was said to have come from Germany, but while there is a record of a Michael Braun's having landed at Philadelphia in 1737, we have no certainty that he was the same one.[11] He is chiefly noted as the builder of the "Old Stone House," described in a later chapter, and as the ancestor of an extraordinarily large number of descendants.

Near the present town of China Grove lived the Savitz', after whom "Savitz' Church" was named. The Rev. Jethro Rumple characterizes them as follows: "The Savitz family were of German lineage, and with the thrift, industry, and prudence of that race, they amassed a large amount of property."[12]

Related to them were the Pfeiffers (Phifers) of Cabarrus (then Mecklenburg). Martin Pfeiffer represented his county in the General Assembly of 1764. Caleb Pfeiffer is numbered among the school trustees of Salisbury.[13] John Pfeiffer was so zealous on behalf of American independence that his dwelling was once threatened by Tories and British soldiers with lighted torches. Just then his little daughter Margaret fell on her knees before the nearest brigand, and, throwing her arms about him, entreated him to spare the house. The child's pleading won the day, and her home was left standing.[14]

---

11. The Rev. Richard L. Brown: *History of the Michael Brown Family* (1921), 12.
12. *History of Rowan County* (Salisbury, 1881), 261.
13. C. R., XXIV, 690.
14. Rumple, 289.

Colonel George Henry Berger (Barger) was a trustee of the academy,[15] and a member of the Committee of Safety,[16] and something of a local Revolutionary hero. Later he was a member of the State Assembly[17] and also a delegate to the Convention of 1789.[18] He was likewise prominent in church affairs, having taken part in the building of both Organ and Lowerstone.

Captain John Paul Behringer (Barringer), likewise of Cabarrus, entertained Governor Tryon in 1768, and the latter referred to him as a "gallant Dutchman." Of course, Tryon could not know that the same man who served him such excellent wine then was later to win lasting fame as a leader in the struggle against British tyranny.[19] Matthias Barringer was the third one of the three Germans serving on the Committee of Safety.[20]

In regard to German names in Rowan and Cabarrus, it is interesting to note the list of those who are mentioned in the church-book of Organ as having begun building the stone house of worship in 1774, namely: Georg Ludwig Siffert (George Lewis Sif-

---

15. C. R., XXIV, 690.
16. Ibid., X, 279 f.
17. Ibid., XVII, 307, 316.
18. Ibid., XXII, 38.
19. Bernheim, 248. Tryon wrote approvingly of Barringer's "beautiful plantation" and wealth of "good hay" (C. R., VII, 821 f.).
20. C. R., X, 279 f.

ord), Wendel Miller, Peter Edelmann (Eddleman), Johannes Steigerwalt (John Stirewalt), Michael Guthmann, (Goodman), Christoph Bless (Christopher Pless), Leonhard Siffert (Leonard Sifford), Jacob Klein (Cline), Anton Kuhn (Anthony Koon), Georg Heinrich Berger (George Henry Barger, mentioned above), Christoph Guthmann (Christopher Goodman), Johannes Rintelmann (John Rendleman), Johannes Eckel (John Eagle), Bastian Lenz (Bostian Lentz), Jacob Benz (Bentz), Georg Eckel (George Eagle), Franz Oberkirsch (Francis Overcash), Johannes Jose (John Josey), and Heinrich (Henry) Wenzel.

To these names we may add the following list, which is typical, but by no means exhaustive: Agner, Albrecht (Albright), Balch (Black), Bas(s)inger, Bast (Bost), Bengel (Bangle), Bernhardt, Biber (Beaver), Boger, Buehler (Peeler), Diehl (Deal), E(a)rnhardt, Eisenhauer (Isenhour), Eller, Frick, Fries (Freeze), Gruss (Cruse), Hafner (Hofner), Hahn, Harnberger (Honbarger), Hauck (Houck), Heilig, Henkel (Hinkle), Holzhauser (Holshouser), Jost (Yost), Jung (Young), Kaubel (Cauble), Kern(s), Kesler, Ketner, Kluttz, Knupp (Canup), Kohlmann (Coleman), Kress (Cress), Lang (Long), Layrle (Lyerly), Lingel (Lingle), Linn, Lippert (Lippard), Loeffler (Lefler), Mauney, Maurer (Mowery), Meissenheimer (Misenheimer), Meyer (Myers), Nussmann (Nussman), Obermann (Overman), Paulus (Powlas), Poole,[21] Propst, Reiblin (Ribelin), Reimer (Rimer), Reitenhauer (Ridenhour), Reinhardt (Rinehart), Richter (Ritchie), Rinck (Rink), Rosenmann (Roseman), Rothrock, Sauer (Sowers), Schaeffer (Shepherd, Shaver), Schenck, Scherb (Sharp), Schluppe (Sloop), Schuh (Shoe), Schupping (Shuping), Schwarzwaelder (Blackwelder), Schwenk (Swink), Sechler, Seip (Sipes), Seitz (Sides), Seyfried (Safrit), Stauch (Stokes), Suther, Trautmann (Troutman), Trexler, Wagner (Wagoner), Walcher (Walker), Weber (Weaver), Wehrle (Whirlow), Weinkauff (Winecoff), Weiss (White), Wilhelm.

It will be observed that some names have kept their original form, while the greater part became Anglicized, at least in their spelling. Still others were translated: e. g., Zimmermann sometimes became Carpenter; Schneider was changed to Taylor, etc. Joseph Nixon[22] cites a striking instance in Lincoln County: an old gentleman named Klein had great-grandchildren who signed themselves, resp., Peter Klein, John Kline, Jacob Cline, John Small, George Little, and William Short.

If the local German population mostly remained quietly on the farm, there was one outside interest that lay close to the hearts of the Palatines: their

21. German spelling uncertain.
22. *The German Settlers in Lincoln County and Western North Carolina* (Chapel Hill, 1911), 34.

church, which they loved with all the fervor of those who have been willing to endure persecution for the sake of their religion. Almost without exception they were either Lutheran or Reformed. They brought their Bibles and books of worship with them, and they were not long in building a log church, also used as a schoolhouse. The earliest arrivals among the Germans seldom had a chance to hear a sermon by an ordained minister, but they held services regularly under the direction of a lay-reader, often the teacher, for schoolmasters were easier to find than preachers.[23] Since the life of the Germans centered largely around their church, it can be considered their most fundamental social institution. Therefore, their establishment of the Lutheran and the Reformed faith in their new home is the theme of the succeeding chapters.

23. Cf. Bernheim, 154.

# CHAPTER III

## LUTHERAN HEROES

About twelve miles southeast of Salisbury, on the Mt. Pleasant road, stands the most impressive monument ever raised to Lutheranism in North Carolina. It is Zion Church, known to everyone as "Old Organ," a structure of massive, uncut stone, obviously brought with difficulty from a considerable distance. Twenty years of often-interrupted labor, arduous but loving, came to an end in 1794—a date inscribed far up on one of the gable ends.[1] The outside walls measure 50 x 40 feet and rise to a height of two stories. Originally there was a high, goblet-shaped pulpit with a winding staircase leading up to it and a sounding-board overhead. On three sides are galleries; the one facing the chancel held for many years the pipe organ which gave the church its popular name. That unique instrument—now unfortunately lost—was built, according to the best information available, by Johannes Steigerwalt (John Stirewalt) the Younger (1769-1828),[2] who came from Penn-

---

1. It was begun in 1774, according to an entry made in the German church-book by C. A. G. Storch. Probably very little was actually accomplished until after the Revolution, well toward 1790.

2. From a personal letter from the Rev. M. L. Stirewalt, D.D.

sylvania as a child with the family, and who later built the "Old Brick House," several miles away.

This is the third sanctuary of a congregation organized not long after 1747. The first one was a log meeting house, situated where St. Peter's Church is now,[3] some seven miles from Organ. It was used jointly by Lutherans and Reformed, but since the land had never been deeded to either group, both presently abandoned it. The second seat of worship was also of logs and occupied a site just back of the present stone edifice described above. After the completion of the latter, the wooden building was used for many years as a schoolhouse.

At almost the same time as Organ, two other German Lutheran congregations were organized, namely, St. John's in Salisbury and St. John's in Cabarrus. These three are the original "mother-churches" in this part of the State, since all other Lutheran groups stem from them.

The Salisbury church stood on the plot of ground now known as the Old Lutheran Graveyard. In 1768 John Lewis Beard deeded the land to the congregation, already in existence for some years; the agreement was that enough space should be reserved for a church, and the rest should be used as a cemetery,

3. A granite shaft marks the spot where that so-called "Hickory Church" stood.

## ORGAN CHURCH

Originally called "Zion," it derives its more familiar name from the pipe organ made for it by Johannes Steigerwalt (John Stirewalt). Completed in 1794, this is the third house of worship of a Lutheran congregation formed nearly two centuries ago.

since a lately deceased daughter of Mr. Beard was already interred there.[4]

St. John's in Cabarrus, three miles west of Mt. Pleasant, was originally called "Buffalo Creek Church," because the first meeting-house was located near that stream, some distance east of the present churchyard. It was of logs, like the second building, which stood half a mile from the final site. Both houses were used jointly by the Lutheran and Reformed congregations until their peaceful separation in 1771.[5] Then a third church was built (in what is now the graveyard), largely at the expense of the most distinguished member, Captain John Paul Barringer. His appreciative fellow-worshipers later had a large elevated and enclosed pew made for him and his family. Three other members, Jacob Fegert, Marx Haus, and Jacob Thieme, paid fifty shillings for 100 acres of government land and entered it in trust for the congregation.[6] This tract still serves as the parsonage farm. Still a fourth church was erected in 1784-1785. The fifth—and present—building dates from 1845. It is a roomy and substantial brick structure, which was remodeled in 1888.

The first school on record in Cabarrus County was operated in connection with St. John's Church.

4. Cf. Bernheim, op. cit., 242; Rumple, op. cit., 350.
5. G. D. Bernheim, D.D., and Geo. H. Cox, D.D.: *History of the Evangelical Lutheran Synod and Ministerium of North Carolina* (Philadelphia, 1902), 129.
6. Ibid., 130.

It had been running for a good many years before the outbreak of the Revolution in 1775, at which time it had a teacher named Friesland.[7]

Even after a generation following the first settlement, the three Lutheran churches, with their vastly increased membership, still had no prospect of obtaining a pastor; inquiries in Pennsylvania had proved fruitless, for that largest German colony in the New World could not supply its own need of preachers. Therefore, it soon became evident that the congregation in Carolina would have to look to the Fatherland for help. Accordingly, the members of Organ Church and St. John's (Cabarrus), representing about sixty families,[8] resolved to send delegates to Germany to secure a minister of their own language and faith, as well as a schoolteacher and a certain amount of financial and material aid. Books of worship were especially desired. Application was to be made to the Hanoverian Consistory, since King George III of England was also Elector of Hanover.

In 1772 Christopher Rintelmann, of Organ, and Christopher Layrle, of St. John's, set out on horseback for Charleston, where they took passage for Europe—at their own expense.[9] They carried two letters of recommendation to the "Society for the Spread of the Gospel in Foreign Parts": one from

7. Bernheim, 250.
8. C. R., VIII, 630.
9. Bernheim & Cox, 13.

Governor Tryon,[10] and another from the Rev. Mr. Drage, the Episcopal rector of St. Luke's Parish. The latter wrote in part:

"The union they desire to live in with the Church of England and the kind assistance they are at all times ready to give . . . , I hope, will recommend them to the notice of the Honorable Society."[11]

London, as the headquarters of that organization, was the first destination of the travelers after crossing the Atlantic. The Lutheran Court Chapel of St. James took up the plan with enthusiasm and donated more than eight hundred dollars. The King himself gave "considerable gifts in money." Meanwhile, through the Court Chapel, a call was sent to the Consistory of Hanover to "assist this cause as much as possible."[12]

Thus the way was prepared for an especially favorable reception of the commissioners when they reached Germany. In response to their appeal, the Consistory selected the Rev. Adolph Nussmann as pastor for North Carolina and Johann Gottfried Arndt as teacher. Additional ministers were promised

10. C. R., VIII, 630.
11. Ibid., 506 f.
12. W. K. Boyd & C. A. Krummel: "German Tracts Concerning the Lutheran Church in North Carolina during the Eighteenth Century" (*N. C. Historical Review*, VII, 1930), 91. Unless otherwise noted, all references are made to this translation of the Velthusen, or Helmstedt Reports, hereafter written: H. R.

in case of future application. Beside substantial cash offerings, Rintelmann and Layrle received Bibles, hymn-books, and catechisms, all badly needed in Rowan and Cabarrus.[13] The Zion (Organ) congregation was presented with a baptismal font and a handsome communion set that remained in use for more than a century.

Adolph Nussmann (1737-1794) was a convert from Roman Catholicism. Even while a priest of the Franciscan order, he was known to be no strict papist. The study of philosophy, particularly that of Wolff, and a closer acquaintance with the Evangelical church organization led him to such serious reflection that, in the course of his study at the University of Goettingen and his work at the Teachers' Seminary in Hanover, he became thoroughly imbued with the Lutheran doctrine and convictions. Under the direction of Councillor Goetten he had developed into a catechist of such ability and zeal that he seemed "perfectly adapted to the best interest of a spiritual adviser for North Carolina." When, on the way to America, he stopped for sometime in London, he made a very favorable impression on the German Lutherans there.[14] With the assistant pastor of the Court Chapel, Dr. Velthusen, Nussmann formed a friendship which was to have important consequences for the growth of the Lutheran Church in this State.

13. Cf. H. R., 92 f.
14. Ibid., 142-143.

In London he was joined by Arndt, and the two sailed for Charleston, where they landed in 1773. Upon arriving in North Carolina, Nussmann preached for one year at Organ (near which he made his home), at St. John's in Salisbury, and at Buffalo Creek (St. John's in Cabarrus). In 1774 he moved to the latter place, where he was pastor for the rest of his life.[15]

Thus Nussmann labored for twenty-one years in establishing the Lutheran Church in his adopted land. He was truly its "pioneer minister" in North Carolina. In every sense of the word he was the spiritual leader of his people; aside from his ministrations as pastor, he was their companion and adviser in all the problems and difficulties of frontier life, in war and peace. Amid active exertions on behalf of widely-scattered congregations, he partially supported himself by farming.[16] All testimony points to his having been the most unselfish of men. For example, the Rev. Dr. Caruthers, a Presbyterian minister, says that Nussmann "labored faithfully in poverty and privations."[17] Likewise, Velthusen writes of learning from

---

15. According to the old German church-book, the congregation adopted a constitution in 1782, one article of which placed St. John's under the jurisdiction of the Consistory of Hanover; in case communication with Europe was impossible, the Pennsylvania Synod was to be considered authoritative.
16. Ibid., 144; 236.
17. Bernheim, 341.

others (not from Nussmann's letters) that the latter's "faithfulness in his ministerial office is so great that he places his temporal welfare . . . too far in the background."[18]

Bernheim states that Nussmann married Christopher Layrle's daughter, Barbara;[19] it is not known on what evidence he based his assertion. On the other hand, Dr. John B. Moose[20] cites a Rowan County marriage bond (on file at Raleigh) which shows that he (Nussmann) wedded Elisabeth Rintelmann, the daughter of the other commissioner to Germany. The names of six children are recorded, and numerous descendants are to be found in various parts of the State.

Schoolmaster Arndt taught the boys and girls of Organ for two years, at the end of which time he entered the ministry, being publicly examined and ordained by the Rev. Joachim Buelow, of South Carolina, on August 22, 1775. As we learn from his later report to Velthusen, Nussmann adopted this measure because of his realization that there were already far too many congregations for one man alone.[21]

Arndt was about thirty-two years old when he came to America. He was a native of Goettingen

---

18. H. R., 236.
19. Op. cit., 342.
20. *Adolph Nussmann, Pioneer Preacher in North Carolina* (pamphlet, Columbia; no date), p. 7.
21. H. R., 144. This was the first Lutheran ordination in North Carolina.

and apparently studied there. Like Nussmann, he had also received thorough training at the Hanoverian Teachers' Seminary. With him he brought excellent credentials from the Consistory of Hanover, under date of October 16, 1772.[22] After being ordained, he succeeded Nussmann as pastor at Organ and Salisbury.

For ten years these two ministers served in common a vast territory embracing the present counties of Rowan, Cabarrus, Iredell, Catawba, Lincoln, Davidson, Guilford, Stokes, and other sections. They traveled long distances on horseback in all kinds of weather, over bad roads and forest paths, to spread the Gospel among people who had long been without pastoral care.

In 1785 Arndt removed to Lincoln County and became the founder of the Lutheran Church in all that region to the west of the Catawba River.[23] There he preached until his death in 1807, but he still went on extensive journeys to visit remote settlements. Before he left Rowan, Arndt organized, about 1784, one of the very oldest congregations outside of the three parent-churches, namely, the "Pine Meeting-House," located five miles east of Salisbury and long since known as Union. The original pine-log building stood where the cemetery is now. In the

22. Bernheim & Cox, 14.
23. H. R., 259; Bernheim, 261.

years 1878-1879 the present church was built of bricks made by the members.

During the greater part of the period when Nussmann and Arndt were laboring jointly in piedmont Carolina, they were cut off by the Revolution from all communication with Europe. No more ministers could come to assist them; no books or material aid of any sort could reach them—not even a word of encouragement. Furthermore, Nussmann, as a strong believer in American independence, was persecuted by the Tories and narrowly escaped death at their hands.[24]

At the close of the war he succeeded in re-establishing connections with the church of the homeland. By that time the American mission field had been turned over to an interested group of professors at the University of Helmstedt, in the Duchy of Brunswick. The "Helmstedt Mission Society" was under the guidance of none other than Nussmann's old friend of London days, Johann Caspar Velthusen, D. D., now professor of theology.[25] On receiving a

24. Bernheim, 341.
25. Velthusen (1740-1814) was one of the most eminent Lutheran divines of his day. After studying at Goettingen and holding a couple of church offices, he was professor of theology, successively, at the universities of Kiel, Helmstedt, and Rostock. In 1791 he became Lutheran General-Superintendent of Bremen and Verden. He wrote eighty books and monographs, beside contributing frequently to periodicals. (Boyd & Krummel, op. cit., 82).

letter from the pastor at Buffalo Creek, Dr. Velt-husen immediately busied himself on behalf of the Lutheran Church in North Carolina. Answering Nussmann's urgent call for helpers, the Society sent the Rev. Christopher Bernhardt, a native of Stutt-gart, to Rowan in 1787. After preaching for a while at the Pine Church and elsewhere, he settled for a year at Abbot's Creek (now in Davidson County); then he served congregations in Guilford, Forsyth, and Stokes until his removal to South Carolina in 1800. Highly pleased with his new co-worker, Nuss-mann wrote: "I can see daily that the Gospel truths which he preaches are a vital force in his own young life." He added that Bernhardt and Arndt had been very helpful in the matter of taking care of widely separated congregations.[26]

Upon the arrival of the first letter from Velthusen, Nussmann replied:

"When I received the delightful reports from Germany, I tried as soon as possible to make them known among the German congregations, which, however, required some time, since in the absence of any printing facilities, one is obliged to travel on horseback to tell the people orally. All rejoice highly in a kind Providence which has awakened such phil-anthropic friends who are willing to aid the destitute American Church in its spiritual needs."[27]

26. H. R., 123.
27. Ibid., 122.

Nussmann had stressed the need of a catechism as being even more urgent than the sending of helpers.[28] The result was Velthusen's *Nordcarolinischer Katechismus*, which appeared in Leipzig in 1788. At Nussmann's request, the Helmstedt Society collected and sent a rather large quantity of books, both religious and educational, to North Carolina. One especially valuable lot was for Nussmann's private library; some other publications he was to sell for his own benefit, but apparently he gave them away to impecunious ministers and teachers.[29]

In his long letter of September-October, 1787, Nussmann informed Velthusen of his having been appointed third commissioner of the new academy of Salisbury. He was associated in that capacity with the "Prophet of Zion-Parnassus," the Rev. Samuel Eusebius McCorkle, whom he described as "a very affable Presbyterian minister." Through Nussmann, McCorkle requested Velthusen and the academy at Helmstedt to furnish a good book on the work of the Germans schools,[30] which even then were models of educational efficiency.

On November 12, 1788, Nussmann wrote Velthusen as follows: " . . . A book-printing establishment would be of the greatest benefit to religion, and we could readily obtain assistance here, if we

28. Ibid., 92.
29. Bernheim, 342.
30. H. R., 124.

only had the type . . . There is no German printing office from Georgia to Maryland, and not even a good English one in North Carolina . . . An organ is also necessary, as it must be our chief concern to reinstate church music . . . "[31]

The year 1788 saw the advent of Pastor Nussmann's ablest colleague, the Rev. Carl August Gottlieb Storch (1764-1831), who had been educated at Helmstedt and ordained there by Dr. Velthusen. Concerning Storch's acceptance of the North Carolina post, his preceptor wrote:

"The young man, after due reflection, expressed a willingness to go, and at once made arrangements for his departure, at the same time receiving a written assurance from his sovereign (the Duke of Brunswick) that if, for any reason he might choose to return, he should still retain his claim of promotion in the Fatherland."[32]

Storch first preached at St. John's in Salisbury and at Organ and Union;[33] he soon resigned from the last-named charge, however. Beside his regular church work and his teaching of German, he undertook long missionary journeys, thus following the example set by Nussmann and Arndt. During his first two years

---

31. Ibid., 239.
32. H. R., 109.
33. The Rev. J. W. Meyer followed Storch as pastor of Union. It was one of the first churches served by Samuel Rothrock, who is buried there.

in Rowan Storch boarded at the home of John Lewis Beard, whose daughter, Christine, he married in 1790;[34] they had eleven children, one of whom, the Rev. Theophilus Storch, D.D., became a prominent Lutheran clergyman in his time. Subsequently he lived east of the town, at what is now known as the Chilson place. After seventeen years he moved to a farm about ten miles south of Salisbury, near the old Concord road, where he resided until his death. This was a location convenient of access to his three charges: Organ, St. John's in Cabarrus, and Savitz', now Lutheran Chapel. Nussmann had organized the latter church about 1780; thus it is one of the oldest congregations. Arndt was its second pastor. Then Storch preached there for many years, beginning in 1789.[35]

Storch was long the acknowledged leader of the Lutheran Church in the South. In addition to his uncommon theological attainments, he was well-versed in literary and scientific matters and, as far as possible in his rather isolated surroundings, he eagerly followed the advancement of learning. He is said to have been able to converse fluently in five or six dif-

34. John G. Morris, D.D.: *The Stork Family in the Lutheran Church* (Philadelphia, 1886), 13. (Stork is the Anglicized form of the name.)

35. Bernheim & Cox, 113 f. Storch also frequently visited the Lutherans at Bethel, or "Bear's Creek," in Stanly, as did also J. W. Meyer.

ferent languages. His library contained "choice works, principally German and Latin."[36]

The Rev. Daniel Hauer, D.D., who knew Storch personally, attests to his liberal views toward other denominations.[37] Dr. Hazelius[38] said of him: "As a minister of the Gospel, he richly possessed the rare talent to create a deep interest for his subject in the well-informed, while he was fully understood by persons of no education."

Like Nussmann, Storch took no thought for material gain. His ability, culture, and refinement would have commanded respect anywhere, yet he declined all offers that would have taken him from among the German farmers of Rowan and Cabarrus, where he felt that he was needed most.[39]

Not many months after Storch's arrival the Helmstedt Mission Society sent the Rev. Arnold Roschen to North Carolina. He was born, educated and ordained at Bremen, where he also married shortly before his departure for America. Coming by way of Charleston, Roschen and his wife reached Salisbury in February, 1789, and made their home near Beck's Church, in what is now Davidson County. After preaching in that section for eleven years, he

---

36. Morris, 26 (in a letter from Dr. Hauer).
37. Ibid.
38. In his *History of the American Lutheran Church*, 224 f.
39. For example, in 1814 he would not accept a call to the large and well-established Church of St. James, at Charleston.

was seized by a longing for his native land, to which he returned in 1800 to become pastor of a church near Bremen.[40]

It is from the letters that Nussmann, Storch, and Roschen sent to Germany that we glean most of our knowledge of their ministerial activities. The Rev. Dr. Velthusen incorporated those letters into his "Helmstedtische Kirchennachrichten,"[41] or Helmstedt Church Reports, already variously quoted above. Otherwise, we are largely dependent on oral tradition, occasional written statements of contemporaries, the rather meagre records preserved in old church-books, and the journals kept by Storch and Arndt.[42]

In one of his letters Roschen commends the love and respect shown him and Storch by their congregations. He then gives the following tidings of the two older pastors:

"Nussmann, who is a good and upright man, lives upon his plantation in very moderate circumstances. Arndt, formerly a catechist, now a preacher, possesses two fine plantations, is wealthy, and edifies his

40. Bernheim, 345.
41. Also called "Nordcarolinische Kirchennachrichten," under which title some of the reports were published.
42. These journals, as well as a number of Storch's books, came into the hands of the North Carolina College (later called Mt. Pleasant Collegiate Institute). Some excerpts from the narrative of Storch appeared in the *Evangelical Review*, VIII, 398-404.

people by his life and conduct. We all preach in black clothes and collar, but mostly without a gown, and oftentimes in our overcoats during bad weather."[43]

With regard to his own preaching, Roschen continues:

"I endeavor to make the Divine service as interesting as possible, and suitable to the occasion, but as simple as I can. I dare not make any discourse shorter than an hour, because there are members who ride eighteen miles to worship, and at each church there is a service only once every four weeks.[44]

From a report of Storch, dated May 28, 1789, Velthusen made extracts that read as follows:

"Mr. Storch mentions that of his three charges, Zion Church (Organ) . . . is the strongest and consists of eighty-seven families . . . His congregation is building a house for him and has offered him a loan for . . . buying a plantation, without which one cannot succeed there. He still lives in Salisbury, where an academy has been established in which there are some students who receive instruction in Hebrew from him . . . He has also founded a small German school, that the youth may accustom themselves to a purer German language. He expects to confirm about fifty children next harvest season . . . Mr. Roschen . . . has four congregations and

43. H. R., 246.
44. Ibid.

receives from them about 100 pounds, current paper money . . . He resides about eighteen miles from him (Storch), has already bought a plantation, and is accustoming himself well to the climate and mode of living in that country."[45]

The first English Lutheran minister in the State was Robert Johnson Miller. Born and educated in Scotland, he came to America in 1774, was in business for a while, served in the Revolutionary army, and at last began to preach under a Methodist license in the western counties of North Carolina.[46] He wished for Episcopal ordination, but as that was not practicable at the time, his congregation at White Haven Church, in Lincoln County, sent a petition to the Lutheran pastors of Rowan and Cabarrus, highly recommending Miller and requesting that he be ordained.

The ceremony took place at St. John's, in Cabarrus, on May 20, 1794. According to the certificate, Miller was "always obliged to obey the rules, ordinances, and customs of the Christian Society called the Protestant Episcopal Church in America." This document was signed by Nussmann, Arndt, Storch, Bernhardt and Roschen.[47]

---

45. Ibid., 240. Salisbury was often called "Salzburg" by the Germans (cf. ibid., 242).
46. Bernheim, 337 f.
47. Ibid., 339. Nussmann's signature was followed by *Senior*, a title conferred by his colleagues out of deference to his being oldest in age and service.

Although ordained as an Episcopal clergyman, Miller officiated for many years as a Lutheran minister. He made long missionary journeys and frequently organized new congregations, especially in Iredell.[48] Once he was elected president of the North Carolina Synod, and three times its secretary. When he formally withdrew from that body in 1821, he was publicly thanked by the Rev. Gottlieb Schober, then president, for his long and active service on behalf of the Lutheran Church. Even after becoming a bona fide Episcopal rector, Mr. Miller did not forget his old friends, but took a leading part in a movement to maintain a closer relationship between the two denominations; in that capacity he still sometimes attended the meetings of the Synod.

Toward the turn of the century the supply of Lutheran pastors in North Carolina once more became dangerously low. Nussmann died in 1794; the Rev. Adam N. Markert (Marcard), who came in 1797 to St. John's in Cabarrus, remained only two years; Roschen and Bernhardt left in 1800. These losses were offset only in a small degree by the coming of the Rev. Philip Henkel to Guilford County (from Virginia). Support from the homeland was eventually cut off, as the members of the Helmstedt Mission Society dispersed to various parts of Germany. Although Storch remained in correspondence

48. Ibid., 409 f.

with Dr. Velthusen until as late as 1803, the latter was no longer in a position to give as active assistance as before;[49] it was evident that the local churches could not further depend on outside aid.

Therefore the Revs. C. A. G. Storch, Gottfried Arndt, Robert J. Miller, and Paul Henkel[50] met in Salisbury, on May 2, 1803, along with a number of elders and deacons, and founded the Lutheran Synod of North Carolina.[51] Storch was the first president of the new organization.

From that date on we observe a steady upward swing in the fortunes of Lutheranism in this region. The Annual Report of Synod in 1806, made by the Rev. Paul Henkel, states there were three "joint" churches in Rowan, east of the Yadkin (i.e., in the present county of Davidson), all served by himself, afterward by Ludwig Markert. Credit is given to Storch in connection with the "three strong Lutheran churches in the vicinity of Salisbury"—obviously Organ, Union, and Savitz'. Special mention is made of St. John's in Cabarrus, where Storch was also pastor then. Arndt cared for "eight or nine German congregations," mostly "joint," in Lincoln County.[52]

---

49. Ibid., 355.
50. Born at Salisbury in 1754.
51. Bernheim, 358.
52. Ibid., 369.

The Synod of 1805 had ordained Philip Henkel and licensed Ludwig Markert and John M. Rueckert. When that body convened at Organ Church in 1810, there were ten ministers present—twice as many as five years earlier. Numerous lay delegates also attended, representing twenty-three churches. Gottlieb Schober received ordination at this meeting; although he served congregations in Forsyth for many years and took an active part in Lutheran affairs, he remained a member of the Moravian Church until his death.[53] The same Synod licensed Jacob Scherer and Godfrey Dreher and renewed the licenses of catchechists Krieson and Rueckert.

Such was the growth of the Lutheran Church in North Carolina that by 1814 there were twenty-one ministers in the Synod, including several who preached in South Carolina.[54] The decades immediately following witnessed the organization of a number of new churches in Rowan and Cabarrus. Among them were: St. Paul's (ca. 1835); St. Enoch's, a colony from the Savitz congregation, (1826); St. Stephen's, in Cabarrus, (1837); St. Matthew's,

---

53. Schober (1754-1838), was born at Bethlehem, Pa., and came to Forsyth as a small boy. At the time of his death he was one of the last survivors of the early Moravians at Salem. The Moravian Records contain abundant references to him, including notices of his organ-playing, apprenticeship as a weaver, and his marriage (in 1782) to Maria Magdalena Transu.

54. Cf. Bernheim, 506 ff.

(1838), and St. James', in Concord, (1843). The latter was founded by the Lutheran portion of the congregation of Coldwater Creek, which had apparently been a joint affair since about 1782.[55] The removal took place during the pastorate of W. G. Harter. At the dedication of the lately-completed edifice in Concord, the sermon was preached by the Rev. Henry Graeber.[56] This rapid expansion continued throughout the nineteenth century and the earlier years of the present one. St. John's in Cabarrus is the parent of no less than seven congregations.

While new Lutheran branches were springing into being on all sides, a revival of interest in the church at Salisbury saved it from passing out of existence. That once-strong religious community had declined when the use of German was discontinued, and by 1822 the property was about to fall into other hands. In that year the Rev. Gottlieb Schober, then president of the Synod, succeeded in arousing the Lutherans of Salisbury to undertake a re-organization. During the ministry of the Rev. John Reck, from 1826 till 1831, St. John's experienced such an increase in the number of communicants that the church was finally placed on a permanent founda-

55. Admission to Synod did not occur till 1814. The church officers at that time were Philip Cress and Michael Winecoff.
56. Bernheim & Cox, 103 f.

tion.[57] The present beautiful building is the fifth in the annals of the congregation.

In 1823 the Rev. C. A. G. Storch concluded thirty-five years as pastor of Organ, where he had begun preaching on his arrival in America in 1788.[58] The following were his successors during the period when German was still used (at least alternately): Daniel Scherer, 1823-1829; Jacob Kaempfer, 1829-1832; Henry Graeber, 1832-1843; and Samuel Rothrock, 1844-1866. Over long periods the ministers at Organ also served at St. John's in Cabarrus and Savitz' Church simultaneously.

Lutheran circles were enlivened in 1819 by a controversy which led to an actual rupture in 1820. It all centered around one David Henkel (1795-1831), who had been licensed as a catechist in 1812, when barely seventeen years old. The Synod refused to ordain him in 1816, but continued his catechist's license, renewing it also at the meeting of 1817— the last one for two years. As the session of 1819 approached, the time was changed from Trinity Sunday to the second Sunday after Easter. On the

---

57. Bernheim, 454.
58. Storch was in poor health during his last years, but he was generally elected president of Synod whenever he could attend. He rests in the God's-acre at Organ. At the synodical convention held soon after his death, Gottlieb Schober delivered a memorial address in German, and D. P. Rosenmiller gave one in English. (Bernheim, 481.)

former day the Rev. Philip Henkel, Candidate Joseph E. Bell, and Catechist David Henkel met with seven lay delegates at St. John's in Cabarrus and declared themselves to be the North Carolina Synod. Thereupon, Philip Henkel, solely on his own authority, ordained Bell and David Henkel. The ordination of the latter was never recognized by the Synod. Henkel accepted the censure given him at the regular meeting of 1819, but at the session of 1820, held in his own church at Lincolnton, he and his supporters withdrew and in the following July they formed the Tennessee Synod. One practical result of the division was an English translation of the Lutheran confessions and theology.[59]

In the light of an impartial review of the case, it is difficult to justify the unrelenting stand taken by the North Carolina Synod toward Henkel. The break was not caused by doctrinal differences, although some of the latter grew out of the quarrel, but rather by personal dislikes and prejudices. Henkel's most determined opponent was Gottlieb Schober; both men were of a singularly uncompromising temperament, and the schism prompted David and Philip Henkel to repudiate their hitherto active endorsement of Schober's book, *Luther*[60] (containing, in brief, a history of the Reformation and of the Lutheran Church in America; the Augsburg Confession;

59. Bernheim, 445 f.
60. Ibid., 432 ff.

the constitution and rules of the N. C. Synod; extracts from Luther's writings, etc., all in English).

David Henkel's formal education was very limited when he began to preach, but his hard study and innate love of books eventually made him proficient not only in German and English,[61] but also in the ancient languages as well as theology. Bernheim characterizes him as "the best-informed candidate for the ministry the North Carolina Synod had at that time." Even then his influence in the Church was considerable.[62] After the formation of the Tennessee Synod he organized several congregations in this immediate territory, among them that of his adherents at Savitz' Church, who a few years later founded Mt. Moriah, near the present town of Landis. He died at the age of thirty-six, leaving a wife and seven children. His personality and preaching made such an impression on the countryside that his fame has lived more than a century after him. Among the stories handed down is the following:

At a certain small chapel in south central Rowan, then used jointly by congregations of the North Carolina and Tennessee Synods and the Reformed Church, there gathered one Sunday a great multi-

---

61. W. H. Gehrke ("Transition · from the German to the English Language," *N. C. Historical Review*, XII, 1935, p. 15.) says "Henkel . . . probably wrote a more facile English than any other German pastor in the State."
62. Bernheim, 442.

tude, regardless of religious affiliation, because the Rev. David Henkel himself was to preach. As there was no room inside for such a crowd, and since it was a warm afternoon in late fall, Mr. Henkel held forth under a big walnut tree, the subject of his sermon being the differences among the three sects. Presently he picked up a walnut and said:

"This walnut will illustrate my meaning. The outer shell represents the Reformed Church, which is farthest from the truth. The inner covering symbolizes the North Carolina Synod, which is nearer the truth, but not the truth itself. Now I shall crack this shell and show you the nut, which represents the pure truth of God's word, as exemplified by the Tennessee Synod."

He cracked the shell and held up the nut for all to see. It was rotten.

# CHAPTER IV

## THE GERMAN REFORMED CHURCH
## AND ITS BUILDERS

From the preceding chapter it is evident that the Lutheran and German Reformed families, having settled in the same community, frequently had a joint church, where they worshiped on alternate Sundays. Apparently the two denominations generally lived side by side in considerable harmony. Just as the Lutherans followed the catechetical precepts of Luther, so the Reformed adherents had their "Heidelberg Catechism." A striking point of variance between the two sects is the attitude toward the sacrament: whereas the Lutherans believe that the participants at the communion eat the body of Christ transmuted into bread, the Reformed Church avers that the wafer is merely a symbol. Such matters of doctrine, however, do not appear to have caused much dissension in the early days about here. Thus the Rev. William Welker, himself a Reformed minister, wrote:[1]

"The members of these churches are . . . greatly intermarried, so that passing from one communion to the other has never been a difficult question. In-

---

1. *Early German Reformed Settlements in North Carolina* (Colonial Records of N. C. VIII: Appendix, p. 730).

deed, they did not make any account of the confessional differences."

Welker states further that a Reformed ministerial student once studied theology under the Lutheran minister Storch. The latter is said likewise to have indoctrinated a class of catechumens in the Heidelberg Catechism and to have confirmed them as members of the Reformed Church.[2]

There is also the story of how, in the days when German was still in general use, one man asked another: "What is the real difference between the two denominations, anyway?"—"Why," said the other, "it is all in the way they begin the Lord's Prayer: the one says 'Unser Vater', and the other 'Vater Unser'."

At all events, these two religious groups were alike in their steadfast devotion to their faith. Just as the Lutherans had to wait a generation before securing a pastor, so the Reformed congregations were for long years deprived of ministers. Pennsylvania could afford little help, since there were not enough Reformed preachers to meet the needs of that province.[3] Even so there were clergymen of that denomination preaching in this section considerably earlier than the arrival of Nussmann and Arndt. In the absence of any pastor, the worshipers were dependent upon lay readers. Both churches used a *Gemeinschaftliches*

2. Ibid., 731. The theological candidate was George Boger, of whom an account is given further on in this chapter.
3. Ibid., 732.

*Gesangbuch,* or "Union Hymnal," published by Christoph Sauer at Germantown.

Among the German Reformed churches in this section of North Carolina, the oldest are Leonard's (or Pilgrim) and Beck's churches, in Davidson County, and Lowerstone, in southeastern Rowan.[4] The latter may be styled the ancestor of all the Reformed churches in the surrounding country west of the Yadkin. Since shortly after 1750 the congregation had worshiped in the "Old Hickory Church," also used by the Lutherans, and then in a second log building. Then in 1795 a momentous change occurred, concerning which the following fondly-cherished tradition remains:

The Lutherans, having completed their massive stone church (Organ) the year before, could not refrain from occasional jibes at their Reformed neighbors who still gathered in the weather-beaten log meeting-house. Thus a pleasant relationship of long standing became strained to the point of an ever-growing hostility. Just then a happy thought came to some of the leaders of the Reformed congregation:

---

4. Cf. J. C. Leonard, D.D.: *The Southern Synod of the Evangelical and Reformed Church* (Lexington, 1940), 229; cf. Welker, 741 ff. Bethany, twelve miles from Lexington, is probably nearly as old as the other Davidson churches mentioned. All three were "joint" meeting-houses. The date of the deed for 53 acres of land for Beck's Church is 1787, but the congregation had been organized before that time.

they could use this antagonism to get a new church of their own. Calling a meeting of the members, they said: "Let's build a stone house of worship exactly large enough to hold the Lutheran church." Great enthusiasm greeted this proposal, and the story goes that it was carried out to the letter—that if it were possible to pick up one stone church and set it into another, Organ would fit inside its rival edifice like a hand in a glove.[5]

Land for a new church (a tract of sixteen acres) had already been bought as early as 1774 from Lorentz Lingle, as shown by the deed conveying it to Andrew Holshouser and John Lippard for "the use of the Calvin Congregation." The cornerstone was laid in 1795, during the pastorate of the Rev. Andrew Loretz. Leaders in erecting the new structure were the elders, Col. George Henry Berger and Jacob Fisher. While the building was mainly complete by 1800, certain details were not finished until 1811. Loretz, who had been succeeded by George Boger, returned to preach the dedicatory sermon in that year.[6] What had originally been called Grace Church (German: *Gnadenkirche*), was thenceforth known as Lowerstone. Its name therefore not only indicates its building-material, but also distinguishes it geo-

---

5. Having a soft spot in his heart for such traditions, the writer prefers to leave any odious comparison of measurements to others.
6. Leonard, 231.

graphically from the nearby stone church of the Lutherans.

Lowerstone measures 40 x 50 feet, with walls 27 feet high, surmounted by gables with an upward reach of twelve feet. Those walls are of massive stone and range from 32 inches at the ground to 21 inches at the gallery, which extends around three sides. By reason of its height and the windows opening from the galleries, Lowerstone, like Organ, has externally the appearance of two-story structure. Smooth stones formed the first flooring, which remained until 1871. The original pulpit was in the so-called "goblet design," so familiar in the churches of Germany; it had the usual overhead sounding-board, as well. Over the outer doors on three sides are slate-like stones bearing German inscriptions. Another one, to the right of the south door, has a dial-face chiseled on it, with the words: *Im Yabre*[7] *Christi 1795* ("In the year of Christ, 1795"). The clock-hands point to the hour 9:30, indicating perhaps the extent of the walls at that time on a certain day in the year mentioned.

In 1782 Jacob Fisher gave the congregation a large blank ledger for records. This church-book is excellently preserved,[8] and a large part of it contains

---

7. Such spellings as *Yahr* for *Jahr* were on the increase toward the turn of the century.
8. At least, it was still in almost perfect condition when the author examined it in 1932.

beautiful German handwriting. The first name recorded therein is Anna Maria Maurer (Mowery), daughter of Frederick Maurer. She was born May 7, 1782, and was baptized by the Rev. Samuel Suther on October 20th of that year. For the same day is listed also the baptism of David Kluttz' twin daughters, Anna Maria and Catherina, whose birth occurred the preceding September 9th. During more than forty years these records were kept in German, first by Suther himself; then they began to appear in English, which in the 1820's was slowly crowding out the old vernacular.

Little is definitely known about the visitations of ministers prior to the coming of the Rev. Mr. Suther in 1768. Since the Rev. Christian Theus, who lived in South Carolina, is known to have made missionary journeys to the German settlements in our State, he may well have preached to the Grace congregation, although there is no certainty that he did so. In 1759, and later, a Swiss named Martin preached to the various Reformed congregations in North Carolina, as did also the Rev. Messrs. Jacob Schneider and Richard Dupert, whose labors likewise extended to South Carolina.[9] Finally, we may mention the Rev. Mr. Beuthahn, who supported himself mainly by teaching a German school in what is now southeastern Guilford.[10] Beginning at the time of his arrival in these

9. Welker, 732; Leonard, 240.
10. Bernheim, op. cit., 262; Rumple, op. cit., 438.

parts (1768), Suther preached to Reformed adherents in Rowan, Mecklenburg (now Cabarrus), and Guilford counties, receiving occasional assistance from Theus.[11] Two other ministers deserving of notice for their ministrations in North Carolina at a somewhat later date are Jacob Christman and Jacob Laros, who lived for a time in Guilford around the turn of the century. In Paul Henkel's report on the condition of the Lutheran Church in 1806 he speaks with the following high praise of these Reformed colleagues:

"As soon as the Rev. Christman was ordained, he labored in various localities and performed many journeys. He was peculiarly fitted to impart private instruction in families, which duty he performed industriously. The Rev. Laros, who did not labor so extensively, was more successful among children and youth in schools and in catechetical instruction; he was always very edifying in his sermons, and his exemplary walk was an ornament to his official duties."[12]

Capable and self-sacrificing as all these men were, they numbered too few for the best interests of their work. It was not until May, 1831, that the Synod of the Reformed Church in the United States received

---

11. Leonard, 233.

12. From the Minutes of the N. C. Lutheran Synod, quoted by Bernheim, 371.

the congregations in question as an organized body, known as the "Classis of North Carolina."[13]

Accepting Suther as the first *bona fide* pastor of Grace (later Lowerstone), we find (with approximate dates,) the following ministers during the century after his advent:[14]

| | |
|---|---|
| Samuel Suther, 1768-1786 | George Boger, 1803-1830 |
| Andrew Loretz, 1786-1795 | Daniel B. Lerch, 1830-1834 |
| Samuel Weyberg, 1795-1803 | John Lantz, 1837-1853 |
| Thornton Butler, 1853-1869 | |

It will be noted that the Rev. Mr. Butler was the first preacher at Lowerstone bearing a non-German name. He was also the first one to preach *entirely* in English; for a generation preceding him there had been at least alternate preaching in German, with English, of course, steadily in the ascendancy. Butler's predecessor, the Rev. John Lantz, it is said, preached "with equal success in both languages"; he also knew five others.[15] The Rev. D. B. Lerch lies buried in the cemetery at Lowerstone.

The second oldest Reformed church in the Rowan-Cabarrus district is Coldwater Creek. No records of organization are extant, since all were destroyed by rats and mice, but we know that Samuel Suther was

13. Welker, 732.
14. At Lowerstone, as at Organ, the roster of pastors, from the founding of the congregation to the present, can be seen on the wall.
15. According to the personal testimony of his daughter, Dr. Willie Augusta Lantz, of Catawba College.

## LOWERSTONE CHURCH

First known as "Grace." The stone building was begun in 1795 and finished in 1811. There are German inscriptions above the outside doors. All Reformed congregations for miles around can claim Lowerstone as their parent-church.

already preaching there in 1768.[16] The congregation long ago removed to a spot just north of Concord, on the old road to Salisbury, and this present church is called Mt. Gilead.

Bethel, often called Bear Creek Church because of its nearness to that stream, and situated in what is now Stanly County, was a union affair at the time of its foundation. Its Reformed membership was a colony from Lowerstone. Prominent names in this group were: Bernhardt, Hegler, Moose, and Seitz. About the year 1804 worship was held in the barn of one Christopher Lyerly, who subsequently gave "100 acres of well-timbered land" to the newly-formed congregation. Thereupon the male members set to work at building a log meeting-house.[17] A record contained in the German church-book states, in part:

"On the 19th and 20th of March, 1806, we erected this church . . . which was quickly brought under roof and was made so far comfortable that, on the following 25th of May, Whitsunday service was held in it for the first time by the Rev. George Boger, who was our pastor at that time."[18]

Later a new frame church was built. When the Lutheran members moved elsewhere, the property came entirely into the hands of the Reformed contingent. Beginning with Boger, the pastors at Bear's

16. C. R., VII, 821.
17. Bernheim, 402 f.
18. Ibid., 403.

Creek were for many years the same as at Lower-stone.[19]

Mt. Zion Church, just south of China Grove, on Highway 29, is one of the oldest of those Reformed congregations that stem from Lowerstone. The first house of worship, erected between 1780 and 1789 and jointly owned with the Lutherans, is already known to us as "Savitz' Church." The building, which boasted of a coat of red paint, is said to have aroused the ire of a crazy man, who burned it down "because it was not painted blue."[20] Three congregations worshiped there after the early 1820's, when part of the Lutherans joined the Tennessee Synod. About 1835 a general separation took place, and each of the three groups built a new church;[21] the Reformed membership chose a site near the original location of the joint meeting-house. The present edifice is a handsome structure, easily one of the most imposing Reformed churches in this entire section. A number of ministers who served Lowerstone also preached at Mt. Zion.

Another joint affair was St. Paul's, or "Holshouser's Church," so called after Andrew Holshouser, who donated the land. Its Reformed portion was founded

---

19.  Welker, 745.
20.  Bernheim & Cox, 113; cf. G. G. Blackwelder: *History of Lutheran Chapel Congregation* (Pamphlet, 1932), p. 1.
21.  The Lutherans adhering to the Tennessee Synod became the founders of Mt. Moriah.

by members of Lowerstone, probably about 1837 (the date of the Lutheran formation), although it was not officially organized until 1850. In that year the Rev. John Lantz, then pastor of Lowerstone, took charge of St. Paul's, which was situated near to where the present Lutheran church of that name now stands. In 1866, at the order of the Reformed Synod, the congregation withdrew to a spot seven miles south of Salisbury and built Mt. Hope Church, on the old Concord road.[22]

Lowerstone is also the parent-church of St. Luke's and Shiloh, both dedicated in 1871. P. M. Trexler was the organizer of the former, and J. C. Denny of the latter.[23] Naturally, the last seventy years have witnessed the establishment of more new congregations than can be separately treated in this survey.

Of the early German Reformed ministers in North Carolina, Samuel Suther is undoubtedly the most intriguing figure. Born in Switzerland in 1722, he arrived in America in 1739, after an exceedingly long and stormy voyage, in the course of which all the rest of the family perished. Even before reaching England, the ship had encountered such severe storms that it was obliged to remain in a British port for several months for repairs. There the father and two daughters died and were buried in English soil. The

22. Cf. Bernheim & Cox, 132; Rumple, 441.
23. Rumple, 442.

ensuing voyage across the Atlantic was a tempestuous one, full of hardships and suffering that cost many of the passengers their lives. Just after the vessel came in sight of the American shore, the worst storm of the whole journey occurred. Samuel was among the very few survivors of the wreck and the only member of the family to reach land alive. Nearly dead when brought ashore, he was nursed back to health by an Englishman.[24]

While barely seventeen when he left his native land, Suther must have already obtained a good educational background, for he early became a teacher in a German school. He chose a profession much in demand among the Teutonic settlers, and we find him teaching for some years successively in Virginia, the Carolinas, Georgia, Pennsylvania, and Maryland. In 1749 he conducted the German school maintained by the Reformed church at Philadelphia. Suther's descendants have handed down the assertion that he was ordained to the ministry there and had a certificate to that effect. Any such documentary evidence has been lost,[25] however.

In any event, he was preaching in the State in 1768. On Sunday, August 21st, of that year, at Coldwater Creek Church, Governor Tryon (according to his journal) "heard Mr. Suther, a Dutch minister

24. Welker, 739; Leonard, 128 f.
25. Cf. Leonard, 129.

A GERMAN COUNTRY HOUSE IN ROWAN

In the text is found a description of this dwelling, formerly the homestead of Ephraim Mauney, at Gold Hill. Such low, rambling structures were once quite common in the local Palatine settlements.

preach, who recommended with warmth a due obedience to the Laws of the Country and a union of heart to support the Peace and Tranquility of the Province."[26] When Tryon ordered Suther to accompany the Rowan and Mecklenburg battalions, as their chaplain, on the expedition against the Regulators, he obeyed, in accordance with his own preaching. With the outbreak of the Revolution, he nevertheless became such an active supporter of the colonists that he was a target for the hatred and persecution of the loyalists. Like Nussmann, Suther was compelled to flee from his home to escape death. Welker relates how "a detachment of the British army, led by some Tories, devastated his farm, drove off his cattle, and destroyed his property of all kinds."[27]

Suther was generally considered a man of uncommon learning and ability, and in the German communities he enjoyed the reputation of being "quite an orator." Indefatigable in his work, he went, in company with one George Goertner, to Pennsylvania in 1784 to collect funds for building churches. After returning from there, he remained in this State until 1786, when he moved to South Carolina. He died at

---

26. C. R., VII, 821.
27. Welker, 740. From this diary we learn that Tryon and his party lodged from August 19th to 21st with Major Phifer, who lived in the vicinity of the Coldwater Creek Church.

Orangeburg in 1788.[28] His descendants are numerous to this day in Rowan and Cabarrus counties.

Beside Suther, the leading spirit in the establishment of the Reformed Church in piedmont Carolina was the Rev. Andrew Loretz. He too was a Swiss, born at Chur in 1761. Evidently he received a good part of his education at Kaufbeuren, in South Germany, where he still was in 1779. Loretz sailed for America in 1784, with a passport dated from Chur. Having landed at Baltimore, he went to Lebanon County, Pennsylvania; there he married a Mrs. Schaeffer, presumably in 1786. The same year (or else in 1787) he came to North Carolina and settled permanently near Lincolnton. Although his regular charge was in Lincoln County, Loretz traveled all over the Carolinas to visit distant congregations. Thus he preached frequently enough in Rowan to be counted as pastor of Grace (Lowerstone) Church during 1789-1795. According to Welker, Loretz probably did more than any other individual toward laying a solid foundation for the Reformed cause in North Carolina.[29]

As a scholar and linguist, Loretz was also noteworthy. Aside from his remarkable knowledge of his native German and of English, he had an excellent command of French and Latin. He collected a rather

28. Welker, 740 f.
29. Ibid., 754.

fine library of theological works, which were later scattered. Such was his eloquence that his memorial oration for George Washington attracted wide attention.[30]

The career of the Rev. George Boger gives an insight into the manner of education for early German ministers native to this locality. From his own account of his youth[31] we glean the following:

George Boger was born in 1782 and was baptized by Samuel Suther. His father, Jacob Boger, and his mother, nee Loefler, had settled on Buffalo Creek, in Cabarrus. He relates:

"There I went some months to a German school when seven or eight years old. The schoolmaster's name was Joseph Hentzler. When nine years old, I went to school again to Martin Schlump, and when eleven years old, I went again six months to German school to Joseph Hentzler. When fourteen or fifteen years of age, I went to English school four months to John Yeoman."

At sixteen Boger took religious instruction from the Rev. Samuel Weyberg (then pastor of Lowerstone and adjoining Reformed churches). Six weeks later he was confirmed. When he shortly afterward expressed a desire to study for the ministry, Mr.

---

30. Ibid., 755.
31. Boger's brief "Autobiography", quoted extensively by Welker, 748 ff., and less fully by Leonard, 281 f.

Weyberg received him as a student for a year; at the end of seven months he preached his first sermon, being then seventeen years old. Upon leaving Mr. Weyberg in December, 1800, Boger lived with his parents until the next fall; during that time he served' three or four congregations at intervals. In October, 1801, he went to study for several months under the Rev. C. A. G. Storch. The following April found him in Lincoln County for the purpose of acquiring still further training under the Rev. Mr. Loretz, who ordained him in March, 1803, at Savitz' Church in Rowan, in his twenty-first year.

Mr. Boger, whose kind and gentle character called forth Rumple's admiration,[32] preached regularly until 1847.[33] He died in June, 1865, at the age of eighty-three, having survived from early German days in Rowan and Cabarrus down to a time when, in the church at least, the English tongue held undisputed sway. Born during a period when the Reformed Church in this section was struggling for its continued existence, he lived to see it become a strongly-entrenched and growing institution.

32. Op. cit., 440.
33. Welker, 750.

# CHAPTER V

## LIFE IN OLD GERMAN TIMES

On arriving here from Pennsylvania, our German and Scotch-Irish forebears found a country which had hitherto suffered very little change at the hands of men. A few Indians, the Saponas, lived along the Yadkin; other tribes, notably the powerful Cherokees, frequently traversed this region while on their hunting expeditions, as may be seen from the numerous arrowheads and occasional tomahawks that still come to light in plowed fields or in gullies. Indeed, a certain shallow crossing-place in the river became so well-known as a point of concourse for the red men that the whites called it "Trading Ford." The Indians, however, left the landscape mostly in its primeval state. Vast stretches of virgin forest greeted the newcomer of the eighteenth century; today some small remnants survive, but most of our timbered land shows only "second growth" woods. Extensive though it was originally, we must not assume that the forest was unbroken. Partly from the testimony of very old people who lived until recent years, partly from the present nature of the terrain, we know that the first white settlers encountered some tracts of grass or meadow land and some of a more marshy character, with reeds and bushes. Even the wooded areas varied in the size and density of their trees.

The German colonists invariably settled near streams, where the moist, fertile, and flat bottoms could be cleared and brought into cultivation with greater ease and to better advantage than the hill-sides and level uplands. Also, the stream furnished abundant water for the livestock, and there was usually a cool spring nearby, which supplied the needs of the household.

Having built a log house, the settler turned his attention to preparing for the first crops in his new environment. Naturally, some years were required for cutting the timber off large acreages, but the rich earth brought forth surprising yields, even with the primitive farming methods of that time. Land was so plentiful that one had only to clear a new field when the old one failed to produce as copiously as in the beginning. Thus originated the plan of taking in a certain amount of "new-ground" every year, a custom which, unfortunately, has continued to some extent until the present, when the once great wealth of forest is nearly exhausted.

The colonial governor Dobbs left the following account of the local Palatine farmers as he found them in 1755:

"They raise horses, cows, and hogs, with a few sheep; they raise Indian corn, wheat, barley, rye, and oats, make good butter and tolerable cheese, and they have gone into indigo with good success, which they sell at Charles Town, having a wagon road to it, tho' 200 miles distant . . . From the many merchants there, they afford them English goods cheaper than . . . in this province. This year they have suffered much by the dry season, having not had as much rain from the middle of March to July as to enter the Earth two inches, and since only chance thunder showers, so that great part of their indigo is so short as not to yield a crop, and their corn hurt. The air is fine, water good, running springs from each hill, and the country so healthy that few or none have died since their settlement . . . "[1]

The almost fabulous plenty of food among the settlers is indicated by Arnold Roschen, in his account of the arrival of himself and his wife at their new home in Davidson. He relates: "The people from all parts of the country brought us abundant flour, corn, hams, sausages, dried fruits, chickens, turkeys, geese, etc., so much so that there has been scarcely any necessity to spend one farthing for our housekeeping up to this time."[2]

Some idea of the prosperity enjoyed by the better farmers may be gleaned from the following anecdote

1. C. R., V, 356. From a letter dated August 24th of that year.
2. H. R., 243.

told by Roschen, who quotes one of the members of his congregation as saying:

"We have need of nothing and possess a great surplus above our wants. We are enjoying good health and everything is in good order on our plantations; and since we are possessed of such an abundance so soon after the war, we must certainly become wealthy if God continues to give us peace."[3]

Roschen added that persons generally married very young, because they did not need to be greatly concerned for the future. Whoever was willing to work, could shortly have a big farm, and poor people were nowhere to be found. Families were large, having often thirteen or fourteen children. He himself was acquainted with a planter who had twenty-three children born of one mother.[4]

It must not be forgotten that this prosperity depended on one's ability to endure the rigors of frontier life. Pastor Nussmann wrote to Dr. Velthusen:

"This one thing above all I wish and request: that no one come in here who has already married in Germany. It would be miraculous if he did not meet with a thousand sad experiences. An American (-born) wife is in our circumstances infinitely better adapted."[5]

---

3. H. R., 245.
4. Ibid., 244 (Also contained in Bernheim, 331).
5. Ibid., 125 f.

THE "OLD STONE HOUSE"

The famous residence of Michael Braun. According to an inscription above the door, he built it in 1766. Its mighty walls are three feet thick.

In the letter quoted above, Roschen tells of the two modes in which marriages were performed. The first way was to follow the rules of the church by having the wedding announced on three successive Sundays. The other procedure is described as follows:

"The bridegroom gets a certificate from Salisbury, rides with his bride, and accompanied by his friends, to the house of the minister . . . or magistrate, where the marriage takes place. The first questions of the minister are: whether he (the bridegroom) has taken his bride without her parents' knowledge . . . and whether the parents have given their consent. If anyone has stolen his bride and has a license from Salisbury, then the objections of the parents avail nothing."[6]

As Nussmann was expecting to receive some ministerial helpers from the Fatherland, he gave the following information concerning clothes for the new country:

"We wear all sorts of dark colors, gray, brown, and blue. Since we always ride horseback on our travels, the more delicate colors would not serve our purpose . . . A good raincoat, if it is rainproof, is better than an overcoat and is necessary on our frequent travels. Good linen is scarce here and very expensive, consequently it would be good if our incoming brothers supplied themselves with it before

6. Ibid., 244.

they start. They can have shirts made here more cheaply than in Germany, and it would be better to bring their material uncut, but of medium grade and not much fancy stuff, for here we must pay more attention to wearing qualities than to finery. Boots are used in summer . . . Wigs we do not need. We wear our natural hair cut short . . . without any artificiality, without curls, powder, or the like. While at home, we wear thin clothes in summer. The dressing-gown is unknown here. Thin trousers, of wide cut and ankle length, are usually of linen, interwoven with blue threads. Black silk neckties are very convenient."[7]

According to the usual pioneer plan, the Germans built their first dwellings of immense hewn logs, notched at either end for joining and held together by wooden pegs. There was a single large room, with a loft overhead. At one end stood a chimney of stone or home-made brick, with a large fireplace for cooking and heating. The roof was of rough boards split from blocks of wood. Spaces for windows and for the heavy oaken door were cut before the timbers were fitted into their positions. On the Five Forks-Mill Bridge road there is a cabin of this sort, now more than a hundred and fifty years old. It was once the home of G. H. Lipe and is still owned by his descendants.

---

7. Ibid., 125 f.

For the ambitious Palatine such a log structure was merely a temporary makeshift, which was replaced before many years with a larger and more comfortable frame house. The latter was often of a type to be seen to this day on some of the older and more remote farms: it was either a rambling building of one story, or else it had also a low upper story of about half the height of the rooms on the ground floor. As an example, let us consider the original state of an old-fashioned homestead in the extreme southeastern part of Rowan:[8]

The house was long and low, with an ample porch included under the main roof. Being built on a gentle rise, it was high off the ground at the rear. The two main rooms were at either end: the living-room, opening onto the front and back porches, and, across the hall, the parlor, rarely used except for such occasions as marriages and funerals. A bedroom adjoined each of the two large rooms. One section of the back porch was two steps higher than the rest. Opening from this porch and overlooking the garden, was yet another bedroom. From there a little open passageway led to the large dining-room and the kitchen, with its great open fireplace, in which hung a crane; finally, there were two spacious storerooms, beside a rock-walled cellar for whatever required a cool place. At one end of the porch sat the fruit

---

8. The Ephraim Mauney place at Gold Hill.

evaporator. The well was only a few feet away; much of the water drawn was poured from the big bucket into a chute, through which it ran into a huge mill-stone used for cooling the milk. No doubt the well-house had to be built around this stone. The nearby smokehouse was well filled with dried beef, hams, and bacon. Just inside the garden gate stood the old bake-oven, modeled after those of the Rhineland. Like all the others of this section, it was built of sun-dried brick, with a wooden shelter over it. A fire was kept burning in the oven until the inside was well heated. Then every last coal was raked out, and the bread, cakes, and pies (the latter in deep earthen dishes) were shoved in with a long wooden scoop.

Two venerable residences of early days in Rowan belong to the most remarkable architectural monuments left behind by the Pennsylvania German settlers. One of these is the "Old Stone House," near Granite Quarry; the other is the sometime home of John Stirewalt, situated thirteen miles south of Salisbury and a short distance east of Ebenezer Church, just off the road from South China Grove to Rockwell.

The stone house was built by Michael Braun (Brown) in 1766, according to the inscription on the stone above the door; he had bought the land from John Dunn in 1758.[9] Well-shaped, but unhewn

9. Cf. Rumple, 192 ff.

Courtesy of Mr. John W. Harden.

THE HOME OF JOHN STIREWALT

More than half the width of the "Old Brick House" is taken up by
the colossal chimney shown here. The large marble clock-face
on the front wall records 1811 as the year of completion.

stones were cemented together to form the walls, which show a uniform thickness of about three feet. From twelve feet or more below the surface, they extend upward to a height of two full stories; hence a secure foundation and an excellent cellar space were provided. At each end of the house is a large chimney, likewise of rock and built into the wall. One of them is double, having a corner-fireplace in each of two adjoining rooms. The chimney at the opposite end has a fireplace facing outward. Formerly a wooden kitchen stood there. Into this fireplace, which is eight feet high, six feet wide, and four feet deep, a large oven was built.

Originally the house contained eight or nine rooms, finished in plaster. Five of these were on the lower floor. There are portholes in the high gables under the roof. The first shingles were of red cedar and lasted for more than a century. It is unfortunate that for several decades this fine old structure has been allowed to fall gradually to ruin. Only the time-defying walls retain their pristine strength.

The "Old Brick House" is in excellent preservation.[10] It has two stories, a cellar, and an attic, and its walls are twenty inches thick. The nine large rooms now have wooden ceiling over the once bare bricks, which were moulded and baked on a red hill

---

10. It is still in Pennsylvania German hands, being owned and occupied by the A. C. Ketner family.

nearby. New flooring has been laid in recent years, but the original mantels and window-frames are still in use.

A gigantic chimney is the most striking feature, it being more than half as broad as the entire end of the house; a unique design is formed by brick of another color. The three fireplaces—two on the first floor and one in the upper stories—can all take care of 5-foot logs. At the base of the chimney, between the fireplaces, a door leads into the cellar, which is as large as the ground floor and also light and airy, since the back part of the house is built on a slope.

Halfway between the two front windows on the second floor is a great white-marble clock face. A niche behind it once contained the works, which, like the clock-hands, have long since disappeared. The dial shows Roman numerals for the hours and Arabic for the minutes. At the top are some decorative designs and the words: "Rowan, N. C." Just above the point where the hands were attached we read: "John Stigerwalt," and at the bottom of the dial: "This 11th October, 1811."

Where the front porch now stands, there was formerly only a huge flat slab of granite. It now serves as one of several stone steps, another being a large millstone from a water-mill that was once a part of the Stirewalt property.

John Stirewalt's brother Jacob also built a fine house, which is still standing near the present town of Kannapolis. Recently it has been restored to its original appearance by a great-great-grandson of the builder. In his then new home Jacob Stirewalt made a handsomely panelled and ornamented pipe organ, which can still be played. The sound capacity is that of ninety-eight pipes, cut from pinehearts in suitably varying sizes. On either side of the center panel are six large ornamental pipes, which are painted a golden yellow. The organ has a sheepskin bellows, a metal footrest for pumping, and a keyboard directly connected with the pipes. It is believed to have been the first pipe organ ever in a private home in North Carolina.

Characteristic of the German farmyards were the log barns, even today so well known in this section. While the last few decades have witnessed a great decrease in their number, many can still be seen, with a broad driveway through the middle and with stalls on either side. The hayloft bore the name "Oberden" among Palatine farmers. Sometimes one finds in the hallway the old-time threshing-floor, shut off from the weather by large gate-like doors.

The first household furnishings and farm tools were brought along from Pennsylvania, and for a good many years the settlers were dependent on the outside world for articles of iron. Hence old wills record how they bequeathed even such utensils as three-legged iron cooking pots to their children. Wood-working of all sorts attained a high degree of ingenuity. Nearly every old house contains pieces of furniture that delight anyone of antiquarian taste. Wood was the chief material for many less ornamental objects such as buckets, tubs, barrels, churns, bread-kneading bowls, handrakes, and numerous other articles for which we now run to the hardware store. Wooden plows and harrows required considerable work, but little iron; they have by no means entirely disappeared, although their use is now limited. Neither has the old familiar rail fence yet vanished completely before barbed and woven wire.

Early wills on file at the Rowan County courthouse make special mention of things which today we take as a matter of course. Thus some persons made it a point to leave a German Bible to each child. Fine clothing, particularly if imported from Europe, was often handed down from generation to generation. This fact is readily understandable when one reflects that for more than a hundred years the country people of this region were largely dependent upon homespun, since "store clothes" were too great a luxury to be worn light-heartedly. Indeed, only in rather recent years did the last spinning-wheels cease to hum.

Nowadays it is hard to conceive of such a "rough plenty" as formerly prevailed on the better farms.

The fresh, fertile soil, the diligent labor of large families, not yet needing to commercialize their production, and the relatively great freedom from destructive pests, all combined to make possible a wealth of food which was further augmented by fish, game, wild fruits, and nuts. In the absence of present-day canning facilities, huge quantities of apples, peaches, pears, berries, etc., were dried for winter. Vinegar and marmelade were made on a big scale; occasionally one may still see a large copper-lined kettle once used for boiling down "apple-butter." Honey bees were then a necessity for every farm, and sheep were the rule rather than the exception.

Thus, with beef, pork, mutton, poultry, and milk products, beside plentiful grain, vegetables, fruits, and the many wild delicacies, one could fare most sumptuously on home-grown food. German skill in baking was exemplified by excellent bread, a variety of cakes, and many kinds of pies, of which the best were the "deep" ones, baked even today in earthenware. At Shrovetide, called in German *Fastnacht* (i.e., "fast-night"), every kitchen was the scene of a busy frying of a light, crisp-brown pastry bearing the name of the festival. It is made of biscuit dough, rolled thin, cut in the shape of a diamond or square, fried in deep fat, and often eaten with honey or molasses. "Fastnacht" became a term widely known even among the Germans' neighbors of British descent, and it is still familiar to numerous persons.

Outside the home, the church and its attendant school formed the center around which the lives of the Rhinelanders revolved. They took their religion to heart and on occasion walked many miles to services, which in the earliest period were infrequent because of the dearth of pastors. Few rode horseback except the aged and the infirm, inasmuch as they believed that their beasts should likewise have one day's rest in seven. Since the tanning of leather was a slow, tedious process, the members of the congregation conserved their shoes, even to the extent of carrying them, while walking barefooted, almost to the church, and putting them on after they had washed their feet in a nearby stream. So a young man on a Sunday school date with his girl had a chance for gallantry such as no longer exists. This custom continued late enough to be remembered by a few old people who lived down to our time.

Work and play were frequently mixed, as, for instance, at a barn-raising, neighborhood woodchopping, or corn-shucking. Especially the latter was adapted for fun during the labor, since there were always some girls among the huskers. In those rougeless times the red note in kissing was lent by an ear of corn of that color, entitling the male finder to osculatory privileges, if and when the young lady was agreeable thereto. After the corn was shucked, all partook of a bountiful supper prepared by the womenfolk. Sometimes a calf or a hog had been butchered just for that meal; sometimes a wholesale slaughter of chickens took place. The appetizing meat, with its accessories, was followed by a lavish display of cakes and pies; the whole repast, of course, was accompanied by hot coffee that drove away the chill of autumn nights. Still so common in the first quarter of this century, shuckings are rapidly becoming merely a happy memory; like all the other dear old customs, they have fallen a prey to an age of ruthless standardization.[11]

Often the element of work did not enter in. There were parties of various kinds, church entertainments, and school affairs, usually associated with good eating. Community chicken or rabbit stews, fish fries,

---

11. Even threshings are now being outmoded by the "combine."

melon feasts, birthday dinners, etc., were typical of an era when the spectre of want seldom appeared.

There seems to be an impression afloat that the Germans were more superstitious than their neighbors, but one finds little evidence in support of that contention. Many beliefs were just as prevalent in rural communities populated by the Scotch-Irish and English; above all, the negroes were the guardians of every sort of superstition. While there was a widespread belief in witchcraft, no one of any race was ever put to death in Rowan on that charge.[12] Almost without exception the Palatines of our locality were devout followers of either the Lutheran or Reformed creed, a fact which may account for the absence of such tragic consequences as the belief in "Hexen" has sometimes had, even of late years, in Pennsylvania. Like the farmers of British descent, they adhered staunchly to the moon and zodiac as weather influences, and many of their descendants now living will undertake certain tasks only "when the sign is right."

One time-honored practice that has not yet lost its hold is "using," known in many regions of the United States as "pow-wowing." According to a pop-

12. Rumple, 326.

ular conception, an adept in this art can make various gestures, muttering meanwhile some cabbalistic words and thereby cure a disease, or, as the case may be, heal a wound or free a place from pests. Therefore, one person can "use" for rash, while another drives away the rats with much less ado than the famed Piper of Hameln. Oddly enough, such a conjurer can transmit the secret charm only to a member of the opposite sex: thus, a man can teach it to a woman, and she then can pass it on to another man. Although this rite is not confined to the German element, it is an interesting ·fact that the local expression "to use" is a literal translation of the German word *brauchen,* still known to Pennsylvania speakers of the old dialect, most of whom, however, say "powwow" when employing English.[13]

Another country custom that survived until our time is that of masquerading at Christmastide, when groups of young people, disguised in manifold costumes and masks, would go from house to house amid song and laughter. Their ancestors brought this old usage with them from the Rhineland, and its name betrays its origin. Locally it is called, in English,

---

13. According to Dr. Alfred Shoemaker, of Lafayette College, an authority on Pennsylvania German customs.

"Christkindling," which is derived from the Rhenish dialectal word *Christkindle*, "little Christ child" (who brings the gifts). Not many years ago, in the Yost district, this pastime was pursued nearly every night during the holidays. The author has his own pleasant recollections of "going Christkindling."

# CHAPTER VI

## "THE WAY THE OLD FOLKS TALKED"

The local German dialect, of Rhenish-Franconian and Alemannic origin, is very similar to the "Deitsch" still widely spoken in those regions of Pennsylvania from which the settlers in North Carolina came. Once the every-day speech of the Rhinelanders in their homes, it maintained itself, to a limited extent, almost to the present time, and the knowledge of it has not yet entirely died out.

While this language was the popular medium of conversation in Rowan and Cabarrus, it was not used in writing except insofar as a few traces of it crept into inscriptions. In the churches and schools of the early days the *Schriftdeutsch,* or standard literary form was employed. That "High German," by reason of its mainly religious function, had often a strongly Biblical flavor, as may be seen from various speciments preserved.

German worship held its own rather well until 1825-1830, according to the records of the church-books and of the Lutheran Synod. Even so, that body had been obliged to reckon from the beginning with members who required an interpreter. For example, the Rev. R. J. Miller, frequently called the "English Lutheran Minister," served as secretary in 1803 and 1804, and as president in 1812, even though he admitted in 1813 that he could not speak German.[1] Furthermore, there was already a tendency on the part of many young people to neglect their ancestral tongue.[2] More than one synodical convention took measures designed to encourage the children to learn to read German: the Sunday school and secular instruction under the auspices of the church seem to have been quite effective for a time. The clergy had two main reasons for championing the cause of the German language: first, there was a widespread belief that the loss of it entailed a religious decline—a theory to which even Robert Johnson Miller subscribed; second, some ministers whose training and library facilities were German, had difficulty in preparing English sermons. The minutes of the Synod were published in both languages in 1811.[3]

Greater conservatism was shown by the Tennessee Synod. At its initial meeting in 1820, German was made the official language, and not until 1825 was the order given to publish the minutes in English also. At the following convention, in 1826, the Rev. David Henkel was appointed interpreter for several

1. Gehrke, loc. cit., 14.
2. Nixon tells (op. cit., 37) of a man who said that he had never learned German and that he disliked the language, because his parents used it to discuss his misdeeds. He added that a sound English whipping was usually the result of the German conversation.
3. Gehrke, 6.

## JACOB STIREWALT'S ORGAN

The fine old instrument, which dates from about 1821, is in almost perfect preservation and can still be played. Recently it has been restored to the sometime home of its builder.

ministers who understood no German. At the same time the following decision was reached:

"The business of the Synod shall be transacted in the German language during the first three days; afterwards the English language shall be used."[4]

About 1825-1850, the real period of transition, there was a great demand for bilingual preachers. Alternate services were held at certain churches for a considerable length of time. Addresses were given in both languages when the Lutheran Missionary Society met at Organ in 1831. From the diary of Samuel Rothrock[5] we learn that both German and English services were held in 1834 at Union and Holshouser's, in Rowan, and at Leonard's and Swicegood's churches, in Davidson. When the Tennessee Synod convened at Beck's Church (Davidson), in 1849, there was German worship—probably for the last time at any synodical gathering in North Carolina.[6]

There was not much German preaching after 1850, and following the Civil War one discovers only occasional evidence of it. In the summer of 1883 the Rev. Mr. Horn, a Reformed minister, preached in German at Mt. Zion, near China Grove; it was apparently the last sermon ever delivered in that lan-

---

4. Cf. Bernheim, 445 ff.
5. Quoted by Gehrke, 16.
6. Ibid., 16.

guage in this section. Hundreds came from far and near to hear that service. While some were attracted by the opportunity of listening once again to a religious discourse in their native tongue, many more doubtless attended out of mere curiosity, on account of never having heard anything except English.[7]

In the fall of 1885 one Solomon Fisher, grandfather of Mr. James L. Fisher, of Salisbury, while on his deathbed, recited parts of the Heidelberg Catechism in the original and some of his favorite hymns.[8] He is said to have led the German singing at Lowerstone in his younger days.

The dialect continued to be spoken rather extensively in German communities for at least a generation after preaching in the language had stopped. It was little heard in public places, however. Writing in 1872, Dr. Bernheim referred to the rapidity with which the use of it was diminishing, reminding his readers that there had been a time when many negro slaves spoke nothing else.[9] Nine years later, in 1881, the Rev. Jethro Rumple wrote:

"The Pennsylvania Dutch has almost ceased to be heard on our streets, where once its quaint tones of mingled German and English were so familiar. The

7. From a letter written to the author by the late Rev. C. B. Heller.
8. From the same letter. Mr. Heller was with Solomon Fisher at the time.
9. Op. cit., 148; cf. Gehrke, 18.

dialect is gone, but the accent and the idiom still linger on many tongues, and the tradition and folklore of the Old World still flow in a deep undercurrent in many families."[10]

And yet at that very time many people in the country districts talked English with a very pronounced accent. The author has learned from a trustworthy source that in that same year of 1881, there was an old Mr. Barger, still living near Gold Knob, who had never learned to speak English at all.

It was estimated that in the year 1899 about twelve members of St. John's in Cabarrus could still speak "Deitsch" and about as many more could understand it.[11] With the passing of time, the knowledge of the language became gradually confined to some of the old people and an occasional bright young person. The last of those who could read in their German family Bibles departed this life long years ago, and the last decade has taken a heavy toll of the very few to whom the old Palatine speech is their native tongue. Of the four men from whom the writer learned most of the words and phrases set down in this chapter, three are gone.[12] Indeed, that was a last-minute opportunity, for those who remember

10. Op. cit., 129.
11. Gehrke, 18.
12. Namely, the late Messrs. Rufus Safrit, Monroe Ritchie, and Crawford Holshouser. Mr. A. M. Safrit still resides in the Yost community.

any of it at all are now hard to find. But what Rumple said in his day still applies in a large measure to their English-speaking descendants. Many an often-used expression is plainly a translation from the German, and certain peculiarities of pronunciation can be traced directly to their Rhenish origin.

---

The following pages contain all the dialectal specimens collected by the author during his investigation. He has made an effort to present this almost extinct language as he found it. An English definition (or translation of a connected passage) is regularly given. Variations from standard German are indicated; any small deviations from the Pennsylvania idiom will be readily apparent to native speakers of the latter. No discussion of perfectly obvious grammatical principles is undertaken here. Attention is called, however, to such points of consonantal variance with regular German as: a) initial *d* for *t*: hence *Daag* for *Tag* (day); intervocalic and final *pp* in place of *pf*: therefore, *Kopp* instead of *Kopf* (head); *w* for *b* between vowels: *gewe* rather than *geben* (to give).

A few notes on the pronunciation are given below. The writer has attempted in the main to follow the rules of German orthography; where that proved inadequate, he made use of the Pennsylvania German spelling employed by Frey.[13]

---

13. J. W. Frey, Ph.D.: *Pennsylvania Dutch Grammar* (Clinton, S. C., 1942).

# "THE WAY THE OLD FOLKS TALKED"

A. Vowels

1. Long *a* generally has the sound of English *aw*. In most instances this has been indicated by the doubling of the vowel: *Baam, Naacht*. Otherwise *a* follows the rules for standard German, except that short *a* sometimes is like English *uh*: *fa, wann*.

2. Final *e* has been dropped in the case of some words and added in the case of others: *Bichs, Marze*.

3. Short *o* is not nearly as broad as that of literary German, but rather resembles English *u* in *up* when abruptly pronounced: *noch*.

4. Modified *o* (long) becomes *ee*; hence *schoen* is *scheen*.

B. Consonants

(Consonants are doubled to show that the preceding vowel is short, as in *nett*.)

1. *ch* is pronounced just as in standard German.

2. *r* is not noticeably trilled.

3. Initial *s* has the sound of the English *s* in *see*.

4. *St* at the beginning of a word is always like *scht*; *sp*, like *schp*.

5. Initial *w* has the value of the English letter: *Wasser*. But intervocalic *w* has the German sound, or that of English *v*: *gewe*.

Examples

I.  *Every-day expressions—purely German.*

Wie alt bischt du?—How old are you?

Ich bin eensunzwanzig Johr alt—I am twenty-
  one years old.

De Mann is gut—The man is good.

Wieviel Kinner hescht du?—How many children do you have?

Ich hab zwee Kinner—I have two children.

Ich hab een Geess gsehn—I have seen a goat.

Steh uff un geh ins Huus!—Get up and go
  into the house!

Geh du; mei Bruscht duht weh—You go; my
  chest pains me.

Ich weess nett, was ich denk—I do not know
  what I think.

Es is warm (kalt, dunk)—It is warm (cold,
  dark).

Es is halfe finfe—It is half-past four.

Wie geht's bei dir?—How is everything at your
  house?

Arrich gut—Very well. (German: arg gut.)

Kannscht du Deitsch schwetze?—Can you
  speak German?

Ich will bluhe (pfluegen) gehn—I want to go
  plow.

Ich hab gedraamt—I (have) dreamed.

Wasser ziehe, bringe—To draw, bring water.

Bichs schiesse—To shoot a rifle.

Heu mache—To make hay.

Wezze maehe—To cut (lit., *mow*) wheat.

Holz fohre—To haul wood.

Sell is een wieschte Maedel—That is an ugly girl.

A ischt mei Buh—He is my boy.

Uff Widdersehne!—Goodbye (German: Auf Wiedersehen!)

II. *Every-day expressions—Anglicisms*

's is regere (German: Es regnet)—It is raining.

's is schneen (German: *Es schneit*)—It is snowing.

Was is dei Maedels Nome?—What is your girl's name?

Du bischt all recht—You are all right.

Loss geh spiele—Let's go play.

Een hunnert, een tausend—a (one) hundred, a thousand.

Ich weess nett, was zu duhne—I don't know what to do.

*Words adopted from English*

Eppelseider (apple cider).

Grand (as in Grandbuh—grandson).

Kahn (corn or cane).

Molassikkahn (molasses cane).

Kluck (clock).

Squarl (squirrel).

Niger (negro, or "nigger").

103

III. *Numerals*

| | | |
|---|---|---|
| eens | elfe | eensunzwanzig |
| zwee | zwelfe | dreizig |
| drei | dreizehr | vierzig |
| vier | vazehr | fuffzig |
| finfe | fuffzehr | sechzig |
| sechse | sechszehr | siewezig |
| siewe | siewezehr | achzig |
| achte | achzehr | neinzig |
| neine | neinzehr | een hunnert |
| zehr | zwanzig | een tausend |

IV. *Days of the Week*
Sunndaag, Munndaag, —————, Mittwoch,
Donnersdaag, Freidaag, Samsdaag.

V. *Months:* Marze, Aprille.

VI. *Alphabetical Word List*
*Rowan-Cabarrus Dialect — English—Standard
German*

| | | |
|---|---|---|
| a | he | er |
| (pron. like English *uh*) | | |
| Aaje | eye | Auge |
| all | all | |
| alles | always | immer |
| alt | old | |
| Ax | ax | Axt |
| Baam | tree | Baum |
| Bank | bench | |

| | | |
|---|---|---|
| bei | at, with, at the house of | |
| bleiwe | to remain | bleiben |
| bluhe | to plow | pfluegen |
| Blume | flower | |
| Bruscht | breast, chest | Brust |
| Buch (short *u*) | book | Buch |
| Bichs | gun, rifle | Buechse |
| Buh | boy | Bub(e), Junge |
| Busch | bush | |
| Daag | day | Tag |
| de, die | the | der, die, das |
| dei | thy, thine | dein |
| Deitsch | German | Deutsch |
| Deitschlant | Germany | Deutschland |
| dot | dead | tot |
| draame | to dream | traeumen |
| Draamer | dreamer | Traeumer |
| du | thou | |
| duh(e), **duhne** | to do | tun |
| dunk | dark | dunkel |
| Eppel (pl.) | apples | Aepfel |
| es, 's | it | |
| Esel | donkey | |
| Eu | egg | Ei |
| Feld | field | |
| Finger | finger | |
| Fleesch | flesh, meat | Fleisch |

| Fleh (pl.) | fleas | Floehe |
|---|---|---|
| fohre | to drive, haul | fahren |
| Fraa | woman, wife | Frau |
| Frend | friend | Freund |
| furr, fa | for | fuer |
| Fuss | foot | |
| Fiessle | little feet | Fuesslein |
| Gatten | cotton | Baumwolle |
| Gaul | horse | Pferd |
| Geess | goat | Geiss (Ziege) |
| geh(n)e | to go | gehen |
| Geld | money | |
| gewe | to give | geben |
| grien | green | gruen |
| gross | great, large, big | |
| Comparative: greesser) | | |
| Grund | ground, bottom | |
| gut | good | |
| Haas | hare, rabbit | |
| hawe | to have | haben |
| halfe | half | halb |
| Hand | hand | |
| heem | (at) home | (da)heim |
| Henkel | chicken, hen | Huhn, Henne |
| Heu | hay | |
| Hohr | hair | Haar |
| Holz | wood | |
| hips (e) | pretty | huebsch |
| Hut | hat | |

# "THE WAY THE OLD FOLKS TALKED"

| | | |
|---|---|---|
| Huus | house | Haus |
| ich | I | |
| in | in | |
| Johr | year | Jahr |
| jung | young | |
| kalt | cold | |
| Katz (e) | cat | Katze |
| kee(n) | no, not any | kein |
| Kinner (pl.) | children | Kinder |
| klee(n), glenn | little, small | klein |
| Kopp | head | Kopf |
| Kuh | cow | |
| kumme | to come | kommen |
| laafe | to run | laufen |
| lang | long | |
| Loch | hole | |
| mache | to make | machen |
| Maedel | girl | Maedchen, Maedel |
| maehe | to mow | maehen |
| Mann | man | |
| Maul | mouth, jaws | Maul, Mund |
| mei | my | mein |
| Mon (long o) | moon | Mond |
| Mutter | mother | |
| Naacht | night | Nacht |
| Naas | nose | Nase |
| nett | not | nicht |
| noch | yet, still | |

| | | |
|---|---|---|
| Nome (long o) | name | Name |
| Oberden | hayloft | Heuboden |
| Ohr | ear | |
| Pasching | peach | Pfirsich |
| recht | right | |
| rot | red | |
| saage | to say | sagen |
| schee (n) | beautiful | schoen |
| schiesse | to shoot | schiessen |
| Schnee | snow | |
| schnee (n) | to snow | schneien |
| Schof | sheep | Schaf |
| Schuh | shoe | |
| schwarz | black | |
| schwetze | speak, talk | schwaetzen (sprechen) |
| seh (n) e, sehe | to see | sehen |
| sei | to be | sein |
| sell (dem- onstrative) | that | der, die, das (demonstra- tive) |
| sieke | to seek, look for | suchen |
| spiele | to play | spielen |
| springe | to spring, jump | springen |
| Stock | stick | |

| | | |
|---|---|---|
| Stuhl | chair | |
| Sumer | summer | Sommer |
| Sunn | sun | Sonne |
| un (d) | and | und |
| Vater | father | |
| Waage | wagon | Wagen |
| wann | when | |
| warm | warm | |
| was | what | |
| Wasser | water | |
| Wasserecke | water-oak | Wassereiche |
| Wassermelon | watermelon | Wassermelone |
| Weh | woe, pain, sadness | |
| Weibsmensch | woman, female person | Weib |
| Wein | wine | |
| weiss | white | |
| Welschhahne | turkey | Welschhahn (Puter, Truthahn) |
| Wezze | wheat | Weizen |
| wiescht | ugly | haesslich |
| wie viel? | how much? | |
| Zehe | toe | |
| zu | to | |

VII. *Rimes*

A, B, C,
Katze laaft im Schnee.
Wann sie heemkummt,
Duhn ihr die Fiessle weh.

A, B, C,
Cat runs in the snow.
When she comes home,
Her little feet hurt her.

Ich hab keen Frend,
Un ich hab keen Geld,
Un ich hab nett lang zu bleiwe.
Heem, siek[14] mich heem!

I have no friend,
And I have no money,
And I have not long to stay.
Home, look for me at home!

Ich hab's alles g'saagt
Un ich saag's alles noch:
De glenner de Maedel,
De greesser's de Loch.

Best left in the original.

14. German: *such* (*e*).

Marzeschnee ischt gut furr Aajeweh;
Aprilleschnee ischt gut fa Wanze un Fleh.

March snow is good for sore eyes;
April snow is good for bugs and fleas.

VIII. *German Inscriptions in Rowan and Cabarrus*

The dialect was never a written language. Inscriptions and epitaphs are in High German (the language of the Church), but some of the later ones betray dialectal influences in their spelling.

1. This inscription is found above the north door of Lowerstone:

Wir gehn in unsers Gottes Hausz Mit Herzenswone ein und aus. Gott laesset uns noch finden Den teuren Schatz, das Lebenswort. Hier zeigt er uns des Himmels Pfort: Vergebung unsrer Suenden.

—Gnadenkirch.

We go in and out of the house of our God with rapture in our hearts. God still lets us find that precious treasure, the Word of Life. Here He shows us the gate of Heaven: forgiveness of our sins.

—Grace Church.

2. Over the door on the west side we read:

Lasz dein Wort in Zion schallen. Geh mit iedem aus und ein. Wann wir mit Haufen wallen, Wo die Gottesdienste sein, Ach, so segne du uns, Herr: Gib auch treue Pretiger, Die dein Wort mit Nutzen lehren, Und die Welt zu dir bekehren.

—Gnadenkirch.

Let Thy Word ring forth in Zion. Abide with everyone. When we surge in crowds where the divine services are, oh, do Thou bless us, Lord: Give us also faithful preachers who will teach Thy Word with profit and convert the World to Thee.

—Grace Church.

3. The dedicatory poem ends over the south door:

Zur Ehre Gottes ist gebaut Die Kirch, welche ihr hir ansaut,* Von einem Volck, so Gott erkendt Und sich nach Iesum Christum nent, Die auch mit ihm sind einverleibet Und sich die Reformirten schreibet.

—1795—Gnadenkirch—Ende.

*For *anschaut*

In honor of God is built the church that ye here behold, by a people whom God rec-

112

ognizes and who call themselves after Jesus Christ, who are also of one body with Him and sign themselves the Reformed.

—1795—Grace Church—The End.

4. Hier ligt begraben Matteis Behringer. Er ist gebohren in Iahr Christi 1743, den 13ten October, und ist gestorben im Iahr Christi 1794, dn 22. November.[15]

(Here lies buried Matthias Barringer. He was born in the year of Christ 1743, on the 13th of October, and died A. D. 1794, on November 22.)

5. Ihr folget mir und ruhet hier,
Bisz Christus komt mit seinem
Pfosaunenschall
Und weckt uns auf all.[16]

(You will follow me and rest here until Christ comes with His trumpet-call and awakens us all.)

6. Michael Trexler war gebohren den 19. April 1808 und esd gestorben den 9. Dag[17] May 1819.

---

15. At Organ.
16. At Organ, on opposite side of Behringer's monument.
17. At Lowerstone.

(Michael Trexler was born April 19, 1808, and died the 9th day of May, 1819.)

7. Hier lig ich: Elisabeth Siefert, begraben und starb im Iahr Christi 1829; den 3t Dag April und bracht mein ganses Alder auf 75 Iahr und 4 Dag.[18]

(Here I lie: Elizabeth Sifford, buried and died in the year of our Lord 1829, the 3rd day of April and brought my total age to 75 years and 4 days.)

8. Selig sind die Doden, die in dem Herrn sderben. Von nun an, ja der Geisd sprichd das, sie ruhen von ihrer Arbeid, denn ihre Werke folgen ihnen nach. Michael Vesperman. Sein Alder war 66 Jahr.[19]

(Blessed are the dead that die in the Lord. Henceforth—yea, the Spirit saith that— they shall rest from their labor, for their works follow after them. Michael Fesperman. His age was 66 years.)

9. Under diesem Stein ruhen die Gebeine des Adam Walcher. Er ist geboren 1722, den

18. At Organ. This epitaph appears on a new stone with which the old one was replaced in 1925.
19. At St. John's in Cabarrus.

16. Mei. Entschlafen 18—(?) den (?) October.[20]

(Under this stone rest the remains of Adam Walker. He was born in 1722, on the 16th of May. Passed away October (?) 18 (?).

10. Hir ruhen die Gebeinen: Margreta Walchern. Geboren 1771 den (?) Agust. Intschlafen den 27. Mei 1800.[21]

Der Gerechten Selen sint in Gotes Hant und keine Qual rihret sie an.[22]

(Here repose the remains of Margaret Walker. Born August (?), 1771. Fell asleep May 27, 1800. The souls of the righteous are in God's hand and no affliction shall touch them.)

11. Epitaph of Michael Braun's wife:

1771.

Gestorbn Julius 20. Hier leit der Leib Magreda Braunds, ML. Brauns Ehweib. Hat 9 Kind. 6 Son. 3 D. Alt 37 Jar 2 Mo.[23]

(1771. Died July 20th. Here lies the body of Margaret Brown, ML. Brown's wedded

---

20. At St. John's. The date is only partly legible.
21. At St. John's.
22. At St. John's.
23. In the old family graveyard; all in capitals.

wife. Has 9 children: 6 sons; 3 daughters.
Aged 37 years, 2 months.)

12. Inscription on original stone marking Nussmann's grave at St. John's:

Christus ist mein Leben, Sterben ist mein
Gewinn. Das Andenken der Gerechten
bleibet im Segen. Hier ruhen die Gebeine
des treuen Predigers, Adolph Nussmann, in
Deutschland geboren, im August 1739, gestorben den 3ten November 1794.[24]

(Christ is my life, to die is my gain. The
memory of the righteous remaineth blessed.
Here rest the remains of the faithful
preacher, Adolph Nussmann, born in Germany, in August, 1739, died the 3rd of
November, 1794.)

IX. *The Will of Christopher Lyerly*

Im Nahmen der Heiligen Dreieinigkeit, Amen.

Ich, Johann Christoph Layrle, Pflanzer in der
Grafschaft Rowan, im Lucas-Kirchspiel und Staate
North Carolina, bin nunmehr eine geraume Zeit
krank an einer auszehrenden Krankheit, jedoch Gott
sey Dank bey gutem und richtigem Verstande, und

---

24. At St. John's. In 1935 a handsome 14 foot granite monument, appropriately inscribed, was raised to the memory of Nussmann.

weil mein Tod ganz gewiss, die Stunde aber ungewiss, so ist es noethig, damit nach meinem Tode unter meinen Erben keine Zwistigkeit moege entstehen, sondern alles nach diesem meinem letzten Willen und Testament solle verhandelt werden, so uebermache ich zur Stund erst meine Seele zu Gott dem Vater, der sie gegeben, Jesum, der sie erloeset, dem Heiligen Geist, der sie in der heiligen Taufe geheiliget; meinen Leib der Erde und meinen Freunden zum christlichen Begraebniss. Mein eignes Vermoegen soll nach Bezahlung meiner rechtmaessigen Schulden unter meinen Erben getheilt werden, wie folget:

Erstlich vermache und gebe ich zu meiner geliebten Frau, Anna Maria Catherina Layrle, erstlich ihren Wohnplatz in der Stube in Genuss; zweytens das Bett; drittens den Kasten, samt aller Leinwand, und die Kleider, so ich von Deutschland mitgebracht; viertens eine Kuh und dann geht ihr drittes Theil in der beweglichen Verlassenschaft. Ihre Versorgung, so lange sie eine Witwe bleibt, so ueberlass ich es von ihr und meinem Sohn Jacob Layrle selbst erwaehlten Maennern, wenn er sein Alter hat.

Zweytens, meinem aeltesten Sohn, Zacharius Layrle, weil er, wie er sein Alter erreicht hat, eine Stute, eine Kuh und Kalb empfangen, solche aber liederlich verspielet und versoffen und ein sehr gottloses Leben angefangen, ja auch seinem Vater geflucht und Hand an ihn gelegt und zur Erden geworfen,

117

vermache ich einen Schilling Sterling und schliesse ihn von allem aus.

Drittens, mein Sohn Peter Layrle, weil er nun eine geraume Zeit seinen Vater verlassen hat und auch ein liederlich Leben fuehrt, dessenungeachtet, wenn er ein Weib deutscher Nation heyrathet, so soll or ein Haus und funfzig Aecker Land haben, an beyden Seiten der Bucht gegen Osten und Westen. Sollte er aber wider meinen Willen in eine andere Nation heirathen, so soll er kein Land haben, sondern den jungen Gaul und nichts mehr. Sollte er aber Land bekommen, so bekommt er keinen Gaul oder Kuh zum voraus, sondern geht in gleiche Theilung mit seinen Geschwistern.

Viertens, dem unter meinem Nahmen gehenden Christoph Layrle, weil er mich im sechzehnten Jahre seines Lebens verlassen und ein Filius naturalis matris ist, auch seine sechzig Pfund empfangen, vermache ich von seiner verstorbenen Mutter wegen einen Schilling Sterling jaehrlich mehr.

Funftens, meinem juengsten Sohn, Jacob Layrle, vermache ich meine Plantage, Land-Haus und was dazu gehoert, wovon er im August 1787 Besitz nehmen kann, dann auch was er aber gegeben wegen seiner Stiefmutter Versorgung, die in seine Vorsehung gegeben; bis dahin bleibt alles beysammen. Sollte aber sein Bruder Peter gesetzmaessig wider den Willen seines Vaters heirathen, so soll er, Jacob, das ganze Land, wie es in dem Willen entworfen ist, allein haben, er aber, Jacob Layrle, verbunden seyn, an seine drey Schwestern dreissig Pfund in funf Jahren Zeit, wenn er sein Alter erreicht hat, zu bezahlen.

Sechstens, meine drey Toechter, Margarethe, Barbara und Catherina gehen in gleiche Theile in den beweglichen Guetern. Zum Willen-Vollzieher dieses meines Testaments nenne und bestaetige ich Conrad Friedrich, und es soll kein amtlicher Verkauf gehalten werden, als im August 1787, wenn Jacob sein Alter erreicht hat.

Und dieses ist mein letzter Wille und Testament mit meiner eignen Hand nach meinem Gewissen geschrieben, so wahr ich lebe, sterbe und mir Gottes Angesicht anschauen will, in dessen Nahmen ich angefangen den 12. Tag October 1784. Dieses ist eine echte Abschrift von meinem letzten Willen und Testament, bezeugt mit meiner eignen Hand.

J. Layrle.

*Translation:*

In the name of the Holy Trinity, Amen.

I, John Christopher Lyerly, a planter in Rowan County, in St. Luke's Parish and State of North Carolina, have been ill now for a considerable time with a malignant disease, but, thank God, in good and right mind. And because my death is quite certain, the hour, however, uncertain, it is necessary that after my death no contention may arise among my heirs, but that everything shall be negotiated according to this my last will and testament; therefore, I commend at this time, first, my soul to God the Father, Who gave it, to Jesus, Who redeemed it, to the Holy Ghost, Who consecrated it in holy baptism; my body to the earth and to my friends for a Christian burial. My own estate shall, after payment of my lawful debts, be divided among my heirs as follows:

First, I bequeath and give to my beloved wife, Anna Mary Catherine Lyerly, first, her right of domicile in the room; second, the bed; third, the chest, with all the linen, and the clothes that I brought along from Germany; fourth, one cow, and then comes her third part in the movables. The management of her affairs, as long as she remains a widow, I entrust to men chosen by her and my son, Jacob Lyerly himself, when he comes of age.

Second, to my eldest son, Zacharius Lyerly, because he, when he reached his majority, received a mare, a cow and calf, but shamefully lost them by gambling and drinking and entered upon a very godless life, indeed, even cursed his father and laid hands upon him and threw him to the ground, I leave one shilling sterling and exclude him from everything else.

Third, my son Peter Lyerly, becaues he left his father for a considerable time and also leads a dissolute life; notwithstanding, if he marries a wife of German nationality, he shall have a horse and fifty acres of land, on both sides of the creek, toward east and west. Should he marry, however, against my will, into another nationality, then he shall not have any land, but the young horse and nothing more. If he should receive land, however, he will get no horse or cow ahead of the others, but will enter into an equal division with his brothers and sisters.

Fourth, to the one who goes under my name as Christopher Lyerly, because he left me in the sixteenth year of his life and is a natural son of his mother and also has received his sixty pounds, I bequeath, for the sake of his deceased mother, one shilling sterling yearly in addition.

Fifth, to my youngest son, Jacob Lyerly, I bequeath my plantation, farmhouse, and whatever belongs with it, of which he can take possession in 1787, then also whatever he shall have spent for the care of his stepmother, who is given into his charge; until then everything shall remain together.

If, however, his brother Peter should legally marry against his father's will, then he, Jacob, alone shall have all such land as is designated in the will, but he, Jacob Lyerly, shall be obligated to pay thirty pounds to his three sisters in five years' time, when he has come of age.

Sixth, my three daughters, Margaret, Barbara, and Catherine, shall share equally the movable goods. As executor of this my will, I appoint and authorize Conrad Friedrich, and there shall be no official sale held earlier than in August, 1787, when Jacob will have reached his majority.

And this is my last will and testament, written with my own hand, according to my conscience, as truly as I am living, shall die, and desire to look upon the face of God, in Whose name I have begun, this 12th day of October, 1784. This is a true copy of my last will and testament, certified by my own hand.

J. Lyerly.

# CHAPTER VII

## FROM PAST TO PRESENT

The foregoing chapters are principally concerned with the hundred years following the settlement of the Pennsylvania Germans in Rowan and Cabarrus counties, i.e., down to about 1850. During their first decades in North Carolina they formed a more or less closed group, although even then they were represented in public affairs by a few outstanding individuals. In the earlier years of the nineteenth century one finds the beginning of a transition, which came to a head around 1825 and lasted for a generation afterward. With the general adoption of English, the language barrier fell away, and there was no longer any reason for the German element to be backward about asserting itself; the Palatines' change of speech was accompanied by an emergence from their original seclusion. Accepting 1850 as an approximate date for the near completion of this transitional era, we shall now give our attention to the ninety-two years since then.

A long period of progress along peaceful lines was disrupted by the Civil War. That fearful struggle, attended and followed by hardship and poverty, was obliged to make itself felt on the remotest farmstead. Slavery and states' rights were issues far removed from most of the local Germans: accustomed to do-

ing their own work, many families owned no negroes. But, as always, the interests of wealth were
served first, and many a young man of their number
gave his life for "the lost cause."

When prosperity at last began to return, the tra-
ditional industry and thrift of the Germans bore
fruit as never before. The country was still so thinly
settled that there was abundant room for everyone.
Even though many young men left the land for
other pursuits, there yet remained enough people to
do the work. Farm machines also began to appear,
bringing with them the opportunity for improved
methods of agriculture. For long years after the War
between the States, however, most wants were supplied at home.

While some of the sons of Palatine farmers were
devoting their energies to better farming, others
found their way into new fields of endeavor. As the
nation entered upon expansion on an unprecedented
scale, there was increased demand for strong and
ambitious young men from the country, both in
business and in the various trades. In the German-
speaking days the ministry and school-teaching had
been the only learned professions that offered much
inducement to the more forward-looking youth.
Now, with the acquisition of English, the Germans
were no longer barred from medicine, law, or academic pursuits.

# FROM PAST TO PRESENT

The German population of piedmont Carolina has been accused of a woeful lack of interest in higher learning.[1] Such assertions cannot be justified on the basis of historical fact. From the beginning there were schools in their local settlements, usually maintained in connection with the church. Reference has been made in an earlier chapter to the highly significant role played by Germans—both ministers and laymen—in the establishment of the "Salisbury Academy." The Lutheran and Reformed pastors were invariably men of education; many of them went as far as Pennsylvania for their theological study, prior to the founding of the necessary institutions nearer home.[2] As soon as our people of German descent were in a position for participation in outside matters, they took steps to provide better educational facilities for their children.

A notable example of such an undertaking is Catawba College, which began life at Newton in 1851 with two instructors, the Rev. C. H. Albert and H. H. Smith. When their classes outgrew their one-room weather-boarded quarters, a church was utilized. In April, 1853, the cornerstone of a brick building was laid. Dr. J. C. Clapp, who was president of the institution for about forty years, held it to-

1. For example, Hope Summerell Chamberlain: *This Was Home* (Chapel Hill, 1938), 207 f.
2. Bernheim & Cox, 64 ff. As early as 1816, Philip Henkel and Joseph E. Bell established a classical school in Green County, Tennessee.

125

gether during the Civil War and Reconstruction period; then, with the help of one Dr. Foil, he made Catawba a bona fide college. The new classical course was first completed by the graduates of 1889: J. C. Leonard, J. M. L. Lyerly, and M. A. Foil. Dr. Clapp resigned in 1900. Under his various successors the college continued to function until 1923, when, owing to excessive debt and inadequate equipment, it was temporarily closed, while an effort was made to place it upon a more secure foundation.[3] With Elmer R. Hoke as president, Catawba reopened at Salisbury in the fall of 1925. Dr. Hoke proved himself a genius in his endeavors. When he began work in 1924, the resources at his command were an unfinished building, in an open field, and more promises than actual contributions of money; there was no faculty, nor was there any academic standing. Within half a dozen years he made it a grade "A" college with a group of outstanding professors, ten handsome new edifices, a well-planned campus, and an athletic field. Following Dr. Hoke's untimely death in 1931, he was succeeded by Dr. Howard R. Omwake, under whose administration Catawba experienced a continuous growth and development.

About the time the Reformed Church was occupied with establishing a college, the Lutherans were

---

3. For many facts about the early history of Catawba the writer is indebted to an article by the Rev. Geo. T. Fitz (*Salisbury Post*, Dec. 2, 1941).

making like plans. The North Carolina Synod had co-operated with that of South Carolina in the maintenance of a literary school and theological seminary from 1837 until 1855. In the latter year, following many months of preliminary activity, the "Western Carolina Male Academy" was opened at Mt. Pleasant, in eastern Cabarrus, with the Rev. William Gerhardt, of Pennsylvania, as principal and professor. The new institution prospered and grew sufficiently that, through amendment of its charter by the state legislature of 1858-1859, it became the "North Carolina College." By 1861 it was substantially endowed and well equipped. Even the Civil War brought only a temporary interruption to the progress of the college, for in 1869 it was reported out of debt.[4]

Mt. Pleasant was also the home of a school for young women, organized in 1859 under the name of "Mont Amoena Female Seminary." A Mrs. Bittle served as principal, while Paul Miller headed the board of directors. Although founded as a private enterprise, the academy passed under the control of the North Carolina Synod not long after the war.[5]

For many years these two institutions did a noble work in educating large numbers of young people. Among the many persons who taught at Mr. Pleasant, probably no one is more deserving of mention than

4. Bernheim & Cox, 67 ff.
5. Ibid., 72 ff.

Lewis H. Rothrock, son of the noted Lutheran minister. Professor Rothrock had enjoyed unusual educational opportunities, including study in Germany, and his qualities as a scholar and as a man have become a legend in these parts.

When, as a result of the expansion of the high school system and by reason of readier access to fully accredited colleges, the two academies at Mt. Pleasant finally closed their doors, the Lutheran Church could already point with pride to an institution well able to meet present-day requirements: Lenoir-Rhyne College, at Hickory. One of its prominent functions has been the preparation of pre-ministerial students for the Lutheran Seminary at Columbia, S. C.

Characteristic of the steadfastness and solidity of the local people of German descent is their loyalty to the faith of their fathers. Most of them are staunch members of either the Lutheran or the Reformed Church. Invariably the church-buildings of both denominations are dignified and impressive; those in the country usually stand in beautiful groves. The congregations of the oldest churches have not failed to do honor to the founders of their spiritual heritage in the new land: Organ, Lowerstone, St. John's (Cabarrus), Union, and others have repeatedly commemorated the religious zeal of "the forefathers of the church"—to quote the words of an appropriately inscribed memorial window at Union. Particu-

128

larly worthy of mention is the centennial celebration at Organ Church on Sunday, May 6, 1894. Several thousand people attended the exercises held in the beautiful surrounding grove, where dinner was served during the intermission. The Rev. Dr. Samuel Rothrock, then a very old man, presided in the forenoon. Among the speakers were Dr. Bernheim, the historian of the Lutheran Church in the Carolinas, and the Rev. F. W. E. Peschau, D.D., the translater of the German minutes of the North Carolina Synod.[6]

---

In concluding this retrospect embracing nearly two hundred years of Palatine tradition in Rowan and Cabarrus, there remains the matter of calling attention to the increasingly prominent position which the descendants of the German settlers have assumed in civic affairs during the last several decades. To emphasize the growing tendency toward community leadership on the part of these people, we need mention only a few names of families that have come especially to the fore, such as Bernhardt, Cauble, Fisher, Isenhour, Kesler, Kluttz, Lingle, Linn, Lyerly, Miller, Peeler, Sloop, etc. They will be found in the forefront of every progressive movement.

Thus our citizens of German blood have followed consistently in the footsteps of their ancestors from the Palatinate. Those Rhinelanders were poor immi-

6. From an article by Z. A. Kluttz in the *Carolina Watchman*, August 24, 1934.

grants, mainly farmers and artisans. With strong, willing hands, resolute minds, and reverent hearts, they set to work and made their hopes of a promised land come true.

To posterity they bequeathed no great wealth, but rather the heritage of diligence, constancy, sincerity, and withal kindliness—qualities which have lived on to this day among Carolina folk of Rhenish extraction. Among the more enlightened there is still a proud consciousness of that lineage, notwithstanding occasional slurs at the hands of time-serving political chicanery and despite aspersions cast by those who are ignorant of the heroic past and worthy present belonging to the German element in the Old North State. Even as their forefathers helped establish a great country, so successive generations have unfalteringly built upon that foundation; hence the Biblical quotation on the title-page. Theirs have been the world-sustaining arts of peace, and upon that merit they have stood and will stand. While making no spurious claims to once-great ancestry or imaginary relationships with royal or ducal families, they can look back, with well-deserved satisfaction, to "the nobility of labor, the long pedigree of toil."

www.ingramcontent.com/pod-product-compliance
Lightning Source LLC
Chambersburg PA
CBHW031128020426
42333CB00012B/275